Managing the New Hong Kong Economy

Managing the New Hong Kong Economy

Edited by
David Mole

HONG KONG
OXFORD UNIVERSITY PRESS
OXFORD NEW YORK
1996

Oxford University Press

Oxford New York

Athens Auckland Bangkok Bogota Bombay
Buenos Aires Calcutta Cape Town Dar es Salaam
Delhi Florence Hong Kong Istanbul Karachi
Kuala Lumpur Madras Madrid Melbourne
Mexico City Nairobi Paris Singapore
Taipei Tokyo Toronto

and associated companies in
Berlin Ibadan

Oxford is a trade mark of Oxford University Press

First published 1996
This impression (lowest digit)
1 3 5 7 9 10 8 6 4 2

Published in the United States
by Oxford University Press, New York

British Library Cataloguing in Publication Data
available

ISBN 0-19-590042-1

Printed in Hong Kong
Published by Oxford University Press (China) Ltd
18/F Warwick House, Taikoo Place, 979 King's Road,
Quarry Bay, Hong Kong

Preface

In a democracy, even a nascent democracy such as Hong Kong's, economic policy is of interest to a varied audience, an audience that includes government officials, people involved in politics, business people, journalists, educators, their students, and many others. Because of this, we have tried to produce a readable book, while retaining some of the features of a scholarly work. Our aim has been to make a serious, properly supported, and well-balanced contribution to the economic-policy debate in Hong Kong.

Such a book is timely. The comfortable certainties of a policy of 'positive non-intervention' in the market economy no longer hold up to scrutiny. The present government accepts as much. The new Special Administrative Region (SAR) government, tackling the same issues, will face the same dilemmas. Certainly the voting public are looking for a new direction in public policy. But good policy is not made by rushing from one extreme to another. As J. S. Mill remarks, the sun never rises on a new truth without setting on an old one.

To one degree or another, the authors share the view that government does have a legitimate role to play in managing our economy, but they recognize that from this common starting point, all kinds of roads may be taken. Indeed, for any given issue, the right balance between market-driven allocations and other options must be sought anew. Good management of an economy cannot be based on slogans.

It is consistent with accepting that there are a variety of solutions to economic-policy problems that the main purpose of the book is to promote a more informed and active debate of the issues, not to push for any particular policy ideas. If readers, including the new generation of policy makers, are encouraged to take their own stand on these complex issues, the book will have succeeded.

I would like to thank the contributors for their hard work and their patience during a long process.

DAVID MOLE
Hong Kong, 1996

Contents

Contributors

Dr William Barron
Lecturer, Centre of Urban Planning and Development, University of Hong Kong

Mr Christopher Blundell
University Lecturer, Department of Public and Social Administration, City University of Hong Kong

Mrs Pamela Chan Wong Shui
Chief Executive, Consumer Council of Hong Kong

Dr Ho Lok Sang
University Reader, Centre for Public Policy, Lingnam College

Dr Guobo Huang
Assistant Professor, Department of Economics and Finance, City University of Hong Kong

Dr David Mole
Formerly a Lecturer in the Department of Economics and Finance, City University of Hong Kong, now Assistant Registrar at the University

Professor Tang Shu-hung
Head, Department of Economics, Hong Kong Baptist University

Ms Teresa Y. C. Wong
Research Officer, Centre for Asian Studies, University of Hong Kong

Tables and Figures

1. Introduction

David Mole

The social and economic environment that has made 'positive non-intervention' a widely accepted approach to economic policy in Hong Kong is changing radically and rapidly. We can already see in outline a new Hong Kong economy. An economy dominated by the export of services, not goods. A society that is no longer poor living by selling its labour cheap, but a high-income society with a sophisticated, productive labour force. An economy no longer driven only by exports, but one committed to internal consumption and investment. This new economic reality is testing the old assumptions, including the assumption that markets left to themselves will deliver efficiency and economic progress in Hong Kong.

It is true that free and competitive markets provide a wonderfully flexible and detailed mechanism for delivering information about what goods and services people want, and about the costs of producing these goods and services. Markets also deliver well-targeted incentives — countless calculations of profit and loss harnessing human greed and, perhaps more important, fear of ruin in a potent combination. Properly functioning markets get the job done like nothing else.

But markets can fail. Private markets do a poor job of delivering the right mix of education and training, health care and social services, roads and public safety, clean air and water. Markets do a poor job of looking after the future — the quality of life and the prosperity of the next generation. Markets encourage people to keep secrets, when the widest dissemination of useful knowledge is more efficient. Markets do not encourage the production of new knowledge, where new ideas cannot be protected by their owners. Markets are routinely subverted by big firms, insiders, franchise holders, organized professions, indeed anyone who can create or exploit 'market power'. Uncontrolled markets do not produce stable growth or stable prices. Markets do not guarantee a desirable distribution of income. They are cruel to the losers and over-generous to the winners. Because of this, uncontrolled markets do not necessarily support social stability, democracy, or broadly based economic development.

The ubiquitous failure of the market mechanism is not in itself an argument for government intervention. The identification of market failure is only the first test to be passed by any proposal for an activist policy. It is also necessary to show that intervention in the economy will make things better, not worse. Governments are as badly organized and fallible as any human institution. They reflect only imperfectly our collective aspirations for more of what is good and less of what is bad. Government policy is often driven by the selfish interests of client groups, public agencies, ambitious politicians, and their friends. Worse, the market mechanism is a vital and many headed animal. Regulation, taxation, price setting, and subsidies are all invitations to someone to beat the policy, or profit from it. Often markets cannot be replaced, they can only be shaped.

The critical test of a government policy is this: does it provide benefits in excess of the resources it consumes? When an industry or service is supported, resources are diverted from some other activity. More support for fashionable high-tech industries increases the costs of unfashionable low-tech firms. Too often policy makers calculate the benefits of a problem solved, but not the costs of solving it.

No mix of private enterprise and public policy, once determined, is right for all time. Neither free markets, nor public policy can be relied on to provide acceptable economic outcomes in all circumstances. Circumstances change, and with them our assessment of the weaknesses of market solutions and of the ability of government and its agencies to supplement markets or shape them to advantage. The purpose of this book is to encourage such an assessment for Hong Kong as it attempts to manage its new economy.

What is 'Positive Non-Intervention'?

Any discussion of the proper stance of economic policy in Hong Kong must start from the reality that 'positive non-intervention' is a misleading description of the government's current policy. There are a number of important areas where the government has not hesitated to regulate economic activity. Also, as the raw data on public spending as a proportion of total gross domestic product (GDP) show, the government provides goods and services on a large scale.

The government has intervened massively in the housing market and continues to do so. About half of the population obtains public housing at below market rates. Pressure has been exerted on banks to reduce the availability of mortgage finance to restrain the price of private housing. More recently public money has been found to subsidize the purchase of private housing for middle-income families unable to qualify for public housing.

Large investments have been made to support business in Hong Kong. Provision of infrastructure and industrial sites is the most obvious example. In addition, support to exporters is available through the Trade Development Council and export insurance, while technical support to manufacturers is provided by the Industrial Technology Centre and the Hong Kong Productivity Council.

In some key areas, the Hong Kong government is an active regulator. Reforms set in motion by the 1987 stock market crash have left Hong Kong with one of the world's better regulated exchanges. The supervision of banks and insurance companies is well entrenched. Schemes of control are in place for overseeing electrical utilities. Bus companies are franchised. Taxi fares are controlled.

If to this list we add significant government spending on education, health care, and the usual menu of local government services, it would be easy to conclude that 'positive non-intervention' is no more than a slogan, a suitable excuse when the government does not want to act, and a useful cover for its otherwise wide-ranging intervention. Indeed among some government officials, not least the Governor, it is a slogan that no longer finds much favour. The current administration has associated itself with policies to improve the environment, to introduce a universal pension, to strengthen consumer rights, and intervene positively in other areas.

Despite this, there is still substance to the slogan and the approach to public policy it exemplifies. This substance is to be found in three important areas — the government's relationship with business; severe spending restraints designed to keep the level of taxes low; and the adoption of crude and mechanical monetary and fiscal policies.

Non-intervention in Hong Kong has not implied non-intervention in the market mechanism so much as non-interference in business. It has been broadly accepted by government that what is good for business is good for Hong Kong. The protection of workers, tenants, consumers, and the environment has been placed second to the needs of enterprise. The privileges of large firms — the major banks, the big developers, the transport companies — are too rarely challenged. The urban planning system has given a free hand to property owners as long as they meet the general provisions of their leases.

No political interest of equal weight to the business community has emerged in Hong Kong. Trade unions are weak, political movements have not taken root, neither the army nor organized religion have been influential. In almost all aspects of public life, Hong Kong is about business. The policy of 'positive non-intervention' is largely a reflection of this political reality. The recent constitutional impasse has considerably increased the influence of the business community. The democratic institutions that might have given political parties extra leverage over the policy agenda threaten to be stillborn. Meanwhile business interests can look to Chinese officials for steady support for the status quo.

Non-intervention has also underpinned the preference of the government for 'rules' rather than 'discretion' in the management of the macroeconomy. Overall, government budgets are managed to achieve some long-run target for reserves. The impact of fiscal decisions on the level of demand, inflation, and labour markets is not taken into account. Meanwhile, the linked exchange rate provides the simplest possible monetary regime. Maintaining the link is, of course, a day-to-day administrative headache, but hard policy choices and the related political decisions are not on the agenda.

Finally, non-intervention has meant low taxes and correspondingly slow growth in the provision of public services. The most notable gap is the failure of the community to develop more than a rudimentary social security system. Social welfare policy has been confined to supplementing the resources of private agencies and charities through subvented funds and to handing out derisory sums of money to those who would otherwise starve. This last aspect of 'positive non-intervention' is the most troubling. It is here that the debate about the proper role of the community in managing economic affairs is likely to be most closely fought over the next few years.

It is already clear that the new administration set up by the Special Administrative Region (SAR) government is likely to resist any increase in the size of government spending and to slow down efforts to create a modern social security system. This does not mean that the forces at work on Hong Kong's economy and society will cease to act, only that sensible debate about the policy response to these forces will be frustrated.

The Emerging New Hong Kong Economy

Of the changes now taking place in the Hong Kong economy that raise questions about the current balance between intervention and non-intervention, three broad trends stand out: the increase in the complexity of the economy; the reorientation of the economy as China and the rest of Asia develops around us; and the sheer growth in Hong Kong's standard of living.

Since the end of the Second World War, Hong Kong's economy has expanded, if not steadily, at least persistently. The first stage in this expansion, a stage only recently completed, was dominated by the growth of export-oriented manufacturing industries. The range of industries was always uncomfortably narrow, with clothing and textiles never less than about half of all manufacturing. This strategy — growth based on low-wage manufacturing, was virtually played out by the early 1980s. Success in low-wage manufacturing is easy to imitate. International leadership in down-market textiles and clothing has passed in less than a hundred years from Lancashire to North America to Japan to the four Asian tigers, and is now passing to South-East Asia and China.

Fortunately, China's break with self-reliant development rescued Hong Kong from its commitment to a narrow portfolio of industries with doubtful long-run prospects. As southern China industrializes, Hong Kong is taking the path of London, New York, and other great cities before it. Industry is moving from downtown into a greater metropolitan area, while city-centre jobs are shifting to personal and business services.

These changes are also being driven by broad economic changes in our region. The new Hong Kong economy is part of the new Asian economy. The recent surge in Hong Kong's economic growth has been shared with the other industrialized economies of the region — Taiwan, Singapore, and South Korea. The capacity of these economies to move forward has been supported by the spectacular advance of Japan at one end of the spectrum, and the steady development of Malaysia, Thailand, Indonesia, and China at the other end. Hong Kong must find its place in a new structure of economic relationships in the region.

A New Industrial Policy?

The most plausible scenario is that Hong Kong will continue to develop as a centre for business services for the region as well as for China. Hong Kong's celebration of the growth of services contrasts oddly with more common complaints from developed countries about 'deindustrialization' and the loss of manufacturing jobs. Jobs in the service sector are often humdrum and low paid. Productivity growth is slow in services, so growth is slow in economies dominated by services. A shift to services is more often a mark of economic maturity than a new dawn in economic development.

If Hong Kong's service industries are to be a new beginning, effort and investment will be needed. High value-added services with growth potential are only a narrow band of service-sector activity. The services Hong Kong wants to provide are knowledge-intensive and training-intensive. If knowledge-intensive and training-intensive businesses are to grow, there must be well-targeted support from the education system. These industries will also have to organize themselves to make an ongoing investment in training. One key problem will be the preparation of a new generation of executives capable of managing firms with a strong customer orientation. Running an office serving the public is not like running a factory.

While making every effort to nourish the growth of fashionable high-paid jobs in services, it must be recognized that bank tellers, baggage handlers, and waiters will always outnumber financial executives, fashion designers, and accountants. Many service-sector jobs are therefore vulnerable to competition from alternative low-wage, low-cost centres. Hong Kong has a head start in providing services to its region, but there is no room for complacency.

A troubling aspect of Hong Kong's service economy is that it remains based on the needs of southern China's industrialization. This industrialization depends on the same narrow portfolio of down-market products that Hong Kong used to produce itself. Manufacturers have moved shop, but not shifted into new sectors. Hong Kong has become the privileged apex of a broadened, but unchanged, industrial base. The problems raised by dependence on these industries have been postponed, not resolved.

Singapore and Taiwan have not had the luxury of easy access to a rapidly industrializing hinterland. Businesses and governments have been forced to pursue the much more difficult strategy of shifting their manufacturing base to higher value-added products capable of covering higher wages and costs. The medium-term pain of this approach can be considerable. In the long term, these economies can hope to establish industries based on specialized knowledge and a dense interaction of designers, management, and shop-floor workers. Such industries earn high and durable returns because this specialist knowledge and organization cannot be imitated easily and because firms can stay ahead as they learn how to do the job better. In high value-added manufacturing, a head start counts and catching up is difficult. Can Hong Kong keep pace with these developments by transforming the rump of its manufacturing sector, or by pulling China-based operations in new directions?

In her chapter on industrial policy, Teresa Wong shows very clearly that 'know-how' and technological change are critical in Hong Kong's effort to remain competitive. As a result, the government now has an essential role to play. Private businesses left to themselves are not good at producing knowledge. New ideas cannot be exploited by their producers for very long before competitors have taken them on board and the advantage they bring is lost. Costly research and development will not often pay for itself. Reinforcing private rights to intellectual property is only a partial solution. It is, after all, better for a community to share the benefits of new ideas as widely as possible.

In the past, Hong Kong has been able to finesse this problem by relying on the transfer of existing technologies and established business practices from more industrially advanced economies such as Japan and the United States. The price of success in this strategy is that Hong Kong firms now lie close to the international technological frontier. Keeping up now means doing more basic research at home. At the same time, as the new technologies to be transferred become more sophisticated, it is essential that Hong Kong possesses an 'infrastructure' that allows for the rapid recognition and take-up of useful technology wherever it appears. This means more, and better organized, scientists, engineers, and other professionals.

The Hong Kong government should now be engaged in the search for an enhanced technology policy. Such a policy would nurture research and development where it is already going forward, identify and promote knowledge-intensive activities in which Hong Kong might hope to take a lead, and create the critical mass of skills necessary for Hong Kong businesses to learn more quickly and adopt useful ideas more smoothly. Perhaps most important is the need to generate a sense of urgency and excitement about the creation of a knowledge-based, post-industrial Hong Kong.

The transfer of sovereignty makes this effort more relevant. Once the integration of the local, service-oriented economy into its highly industrialized hinterland is recognized, support for the development of manufacturing technologies and for downstream business services can be developed as mutually reinforcing, not competing strategies.

Training and Retraining

There is a second area of concern. The turbulence of the economy as it diversifies places new demands on workers as well as firms. At its current high rates of growth, Hong Kong is accomplishing a massive shift of labour across sectors with less pain than might be expected. But the process is far from complete. Workers will need training and retraining, if they are to keep up with the needs of the economy.

As Ho Lok Sang shows in his chapter on the labour market, this is another task that cannot be left to the private market. Information about employer needs and worker skills is difficult to acquire. Even where they identify a needed skill, most workers cannot finance an investment in training, while employers are reluctant to provide training for workers who may not stay with the firm. The government's current initiatives to assist workers and firms are confused in their aims and ill directed. A clear distinction between programmes to assist unskilled workers whose livelihood has been swept away by economic change and programmes directed at the strategic problems of an economy in transition is still not being made.

Getting the right mix of public and private activity in worker training or in research and development is no easy matter. It is however one of the most important tasks before the community. Hong Kong cannot expect to live forever on the easy money generated by the industrialization of its hinterland. This is a time for wise investment in the future.

A New Approach to Macroeconomic Policy

A Hong Kong economy driven by labour-intensive manufacturing exports responded to international cycles in the demand for local products. The problem of macroeconomic policy is reduced to that of maintaining the convertibility of the Hong Kong dollar and keeping the government's books well balanced. There was little to gain from sophisticated exercises in overall demand management. Hong Kong businesses and workers rode out periodic slumps in their major markets as best they could.

Also, where the vast majority of workers are unskilled, but are able to move fairly flexibly among the jobs offered, wages should adjust pretty quickly to fluctuations in demand. The miseries of cyclical unemployment, stubborn inflation, and 'stagflation' that afflict the advanced economies were not critical issues for policy makers.

In the new Hong Kong economy, conditions have changed.

The demand for exports is no longer the only important component of aggregate demand. Demand from local consumers for locally produced goods and services and local investment to support the production of these goods and services is now significant. The composition of imports is also shifting as raw materials and basic foods are displaced by a range of consumer items — cars, electronics, clothes, and appliances. There is now the potential for made-in-Hong Kong business cycles, and certainly for domestic factors to exaggerate the impact of the economic shocks delivered by the international economy. Given this, there is scope for, and the need for, demand management through whatever fiscal and monetary mechanisms are available.

A policy of positive intervention in the macroeconomy will be complicated by the new realities of Hong Kong's labour market. Where jobs become more specialized, labour markets are slower to adjust. The costs of searching for new work and the greater difficulty for employers and employees in assessing the appropriate wage given economic conditions, means that wages will be slower to respond to changes in those conditions. Unemployment rises, or unfilled vacancies emerge, while the response of the economy to policy initiatives becomes sluggish and uncertain.

In a less uncertain political environment, Hong Kong would by now have learned a lesson from Singapore in sound monetary management. Singapore has shown that in a very small internationalized economy the exchange rate can be a convenient and effective instrument for managing domestic prices and interest rates. However, Guobo Huang, in his chapter on exchange rate policy, concludes that, for now, Hong Kong's linked exchange rate is the only serious monetary policy option.

This is unfortunate. A direct result of the link has been the importation into Hong Kong of nominal interest rates that are inappropriate to local economic conditions. This has led to a chronic macroeconomic imbalance producing a rapid, persistent, and now entrenched inflation. Despite a persistent fall-off in growth and rising unemployment, inflation levels are still much higher than in economies with which Hong Kong is in direct competition. Moreover, as long as the link is in place, there can be no effective monetary policy response to the problem. In the face of this situation, government officials and those who advise them have been dangerously complacent.

Complacency has been compounded by a sense of help-lessness; if inflation is the price of the linked exchange rate, so be it. But Guobo Huang goes on to show that the 'fixed exchange rate' regime of the link provides an ideal environment for macroeconomic management through fiscal policy. Perhaps more important, it creates an environment in which the government's fiscal policy decisions have a profound impact on the local economy, whatever their motivation. The time has come for Hong Kong to grapple with its macroeconomic problems. With inflation comes an erosion of economic competitiveness that may never be reversed, the distortion of long-run investment decisions, the poisoning of labour relations, unacceptable twists in the distribution of income, and an inevitable macroeconomic reaction when the growth surge it produces is spent.

The Challenge of Affluence

While the challenge to positive non-intervention comes in part from contemplating the huge task that lies before Hong Kong, current policy is also being undermined by what has been accomplished already. Export-oriented manufacturing may have meant unstable growth on a narrow base, but this has not prevented Hong Kong from growing richer, finally rich enough to be counted as a high-income community, by some reckonings standing sixth in the world for GDP per capita. A quantitative change on this scale must now lead to a qualitative transformation.

Rich communities have different demands on their governments than poor communities. Many of the luxuries of life are, in their nature, goods that are more effectively provided collectively. This has implications for the government as a planner and regulator, for government expenditure, and for the tax system that supports government spending.

One critical area is housing. Despite its acknowledged contribution to past economic and social development, the scale of Hong Kong's investment in public housing is now open to question. In Chapter 7, Chris Blundell has provided a very valuable survey of the issues. He concludes that there remains a role for public housing in Hong Kong. As he suggests, this conclusion raises more questions than it settles — how much, what quality, how managed, and so on. As always, once the comfortable, but misleading, certainties of *laissez-faire* are left behind, the hard work begins.

The desire for a greener and more spacious urban environment, cleaner water, and cleaner air is another clear example of the changing demands on government. Hong Kong's urban planning system, a system in which the sale of leases to crown land has been the main point of leverage over developers, has accommodated large investments in public housing and rapid private development. Within planned neighbourhoods, both public and private, environmental considerations have had their due. Unfortunately, the wider urban environment has been neglected. This neglect is a legacy of non-intervention that must now be dealt with.

As William Barron shows in Chapter 8, although the government has been in the lead in a number of areas of environmental policy, the quality of air and water continue to fall. Worse than this, in its own infrastructural projects, the government has exempted itself from the necessary impact studies. We are about to make a massive government-led intervention in Hong Kong's environment without evaluating, or debating, the resulting costs.

A community struggling to make a living, as Hong Kong has until recently, is likely to regard worker safety, consumer protection, and tenants' rights as secondary considerations. Workers, for example, would rather earn higher wages in a dangerous workplace than lower wages in one made safer, but more costly, by regulation. As incomes rise, however, the mix of characteristics demanded changes. Safe and pleasant working conditions become something workers can afford. Even without government intervention, there will be a shift towards better conditions, but regulation makes an essential contribution to getting the mix right. Similar arguments can be applied to health and safety standards for goods and services and for giving tenants additional legal leverage over landlords.

The protection of consumers from unscrupulous businesses and businesses with sufficient market power to rig the system in their favour is high on the list of reforms required by the new conditions. In her chapter on consumer protection,

Pamela Chan points out that Hong Kong lags behind other communities in regulating unsafe products and unfair market practice. As the goods and services we consume become more costly and complex, we require full and accurate information about them. 'Buyer beware' may be a useful standard in a vegetable market, but it is not sufficient in the market for life insurance.

She also notes that as Hong Kong becomes more prosperous the balance of consumer spending is shifting to locally produced services and away from imported goods. International competition does little to curb the market power of local producers of services and the small size of the local market invites the development of oligopolies. Establishing an effective competition policy is therefore becoming urgent. The government's approach to competition policy will be an interesting test of the strength of its commitment to 'markets' as opposed to its commitment to business. Its failure to deal firmly and finally with the naked cartel that fixes bank interest rates in Hong Kong is not encouraging. The government is already a busy regulator of prices for some public utilities. Bringing the regulation of utility prices up to the international standard is therefore also on the agenda.

Creating a more desirable, high-income mix of production and consumption will mean more public spending. The experience of wealthy countries suggests that health care and education will be the biggest growth areas in the government's budget for public services. But other spending pressures will emerge — for a graceful and healthy environment, day care, increased public safety, amenities for old people, better roads — the list is long. Private provision of some of these goods and services will also increase. The question will be one of balance. In some areas, the non-market, administrative solution is simply more efficient.

But under current government fiscal policies, finding this new balance for the level of spending on new amenities, training, or a technology policy, is not possible. As Tang Shuhung shows in his account of Hong Kong's fiscal arrangements, the government, in its reasonable desire for fiscal prudence, has established a set of mechanical budgetary ratios that have dramatically limited its flexibility. Unfortunately, this rigidity has now been given quasi-constitutional status in the Basic Law and in the Memorandum of Understanding on airport finance. The most serious constraints are over the use of reserves and the inability of the government to issue debt commensurate with the level of public investment required to maintain Hong Kong's position in the region.

Ultimately, if higher government spending is required, more money will have to be raised by taxes. Positive non-intervention has implied a low-tax economy. High-income communities are not low-tax communities. They need to have in place a broad, fair tax system that minimizes the distortion of private decision-making. Only such a tax system can support the levels of tax needed to sustain public consumption. A good argument can be made that Hong Kong should follow the world-wide trend and shift its taxes away from income and toward expenditure. Expenditure taxes are fairer because expenditure cannot be hidden as easily as income. Also, expenditure taxes do not discourage saving.

The main criticism of value-added taxes is that they fall harder on the less well off. From a distributional point of view, expenditure-based taxes are acceptable only where they are part of a tax and spending system that offsets their regressive effect. Putting into place a well designed value-added tax and minimizing its distributional effect will call for an enormous political and administrative effort. It is a grave mistake to let matters drift; now is the time to begin the process of reform.

The Distribution of Income

In today's high-income Hong Kong, an issue which has been dormant for many years has reemerged — social class and the distribution of income. In a low-income economy, desperate housing conditions, poor diet, high infant mortality, overwork, and ill health are at the top of the social agenda. Affluence does not mean that these problems disappear, but it changes their character. When standards of living are generally low, community life is adapted to the conditions. Shops and restaurants, domestic architecture and family life, business and public services are all tailored for serving a low-income community. As the community's standard of living rises, poverty becomes the condition of a minority, a minority that now lacks the support of a low-income social system. A problem that was unmanageably broad may become unmanageably deep.

There is also a danger that the problem of income distribution will be made more serious as the Hong Kong economy transforms. While the opening to China has been a source of wealth to many people in Hong Kong, it represents new competition for others. Factory workers, workers in low-skill services, even some semi-skilled workers — bank tellers and bookkeepers — may find their wages failing to keep up. Competition from the rest of Asia where wages are low is also growing. Increasing average incomes may be associated with a stretching of the distribution of income — a longer tail of very rich at one end, and a longer tail of poor at the other. There is already evidence of a deterioration in Hong Kong's distribution of income.

For a community that wishes to remain progressive this is a great challenge. Economic development is not a matter of riches trickling down. The engine of development is investment in education and skills, the broadest possible effort to increase productivity and thus income levels. It is critical that working people not conclude that their efforts are hopeless and that the system is rigged against them. Incentives for individuals and families to move up the ladder must be maintained. It must remain a good investment for the poorest members of the community to educate their children, to improve their skills, to work at small businesses, and make them prosper.

There are no simple policy solutions to a problem that has deep roots in the structure of the economy. The main burden is on education policy, including training and retraining. Well designed social policies can also help — affordable housing, quality day care, help with old people, support for children — whatever is required to help disadvantaged families to help themselves.

There is also a challenge for business. When the aspiration to get rich is widely shared and hard work is a plausible strategy for families attempting to keep up with economic growth, 'labour relations' are not likely to be a critical problem. In well-managed Hong Kong firms in the new Hong Kong economy, labour relations will have to give way to human relations. Only where employees are given a stake in the organization and its success will a business thrive.

At this point, a catalogue of policy issues for the new Hong

Kong economy begins to trespass on the policy problems of the new Hong Kong society. However open a community remains to individuals willing to work hard for themselves, there will always be those who cannot make a living. All societies must solve this problem. A desire for fairness, a desire to relieve undue suffering, the need to maintain social stability and preserve open government all demand that an adequate social safety net be in place. At the same time, a social security system that is too broad or badly designed can impair incentives to work, undermine families and finally drag down the entire fiscal system with the expense of entitlements.

Too often debate about social security policy fails to get beyond generalities. The issue is not whether Hong Kong needs a reformed social security system, but how this new system is to be set up to maximize its benefits and minimize its costs, both financial and social. Ho Lok Sang, in his chapter on labour markets, offers some fairly detailed proposals. Before Hong Kong can find its own solutions to these difficult policy problems, a tremendous amount of work must be done.

Beyond Positive Non-intervention

Not surprisingly the pressures identified above are already leading to adjustments in the stance of economic policy. Examples are not difficult to find. The government is moving to strengthen urban planning controls. Health care is under review. A pension scheme is likely to be enacted. The institutions of full central banking have been steadily built up. Indeed some readers will feel that the pace of change is already too rapid and that it should be slowed, not accelerated.

It is therefore worth concluding this introduction on a cautionary note. It is easy to argue for an ideal plan of intervention relative to the alternative of real-world markets with their gaps and failures. It is much harder to have confidence in the outcome of real-world governments to achieve the results we want. The provision of public goods with the desired characteristics and in the right amount is difficult to organize. Getting the regulations right is detailed and messy work. Keeping taxes fair and neutral is a constant struggle.

As the burden of social and economic organization is shifted from the market to public policy, the demands on the efficiency and openness of government increase. These demands can only be met through a political process in which a range of views can be heard and differences of opinion reconciled, and where public agencies are responsive and active. None of this is easy to achieve. It is, however, worth the effort. The policy of leaving markets alone is too often not a policy at all, but an excuse for doing nothing.

2. Going Up-market: An Industrial Policy for Hong Kong in the 1990s

Teresa Y. C. Wong

LS2

The long history of Hong Kong's industrial development has been marked by rapid change, as the textile boom of the 1950s and 1960s gave way to the emergence of the garment and plastics industries in the 1970s and, more recently, as the electronics and toy industries developed into the multi-billion dollar businesses of today. This process of change has been driven by a number of dynamic forces.

Firstly, the available inputs of capital and labour have changed. Economic development has made possible the production of high-technology and high-skill products. Secondly, a wave of industrial automation that started in the early 1980s has gathered strength. Thirdly, Hong Kong industries have become increasingly internationalized. In particular, an inflow of foreign capital has helped to modernize and upgrade the manufacturing sector, while manufacturing has been relocated to low-cost sites in the region, releasing local resources to other areas where the economy has acquired new cost and production advantages. Finally, investment outflows from Hong Kong have made it the centre of new international business networks.

Current trends in industrial development suggest that significant changes are in prospect for the future. It is anticipated that Hong Kong will continue to upgrade its traditional industries, while developing new industries. Manufacturing activities in Hong Kong will continue to move up-market, concentrating more and more on quality and precision, while the share of manufacturing in the economy will shrink as a result of the relocation of manufacturing activities. The old manufacturing base will convert more and more to 'manufacturing related' activities, activities that are design-conscious and customer-oriented. From a regional perspective, production and trading relationships among Hong Kong, South

China, and Taiwan will get closer, with Hong Kong ultimately integrating with the Pearl River Delta, and Taiwan with Fujian Province. Ultimately the South China Economic Zone will become a huge manufacturing base, with its member countries sharing markets, natural resources, technology, and manpower.

The changing role of the Hong Kong manufacturing sector, and the move toward more up-market products, raises an important policy question — should the economy's industrial policy also move up-market?

The economic recession between 1974 and 1976 increased both private and public awareness of the importance of stronger support, and clearer guidance from the government to assist industry to upgrade and diversify. Since then, there has been pressure from businessmen and academia for the government to formulate a more vigorous set of industrial policies. In 1979, an Advisory Committee appointed by the government published the *Report of the Advisory Committee on Diversification*. The Report represented a landmark in the development of Hong Kong's industrial policy. It suggested a more active public attitude to industrial development, and outlined the objectives which should be attained in future.

In characterizing Hong Kong's current policy position a useful comparison can be made with Singapore. Hong Kong's industrial policy is basically educational, infrastructural, and service oriented. That of Singapore is basically fiscal and financial. Furthermore, the Hong Kong government approaches industrial development by maintaining the economy's locational advantages, while the Singapore government approaches industrialization by influencing industrial structure, including the choice of industries and the choice of technology.

In view of the rapid changes in industrial development, both locally and in the region, the main issue is no longer whether Hong Kong needs an active industrial policy. The prominent issues are, firstly, should Hong Kong's industrial policy now go beyond what was outlined in the 1979 Report? Secondly, if a new approach is called for, what new policies should be developed? This chapter is concerned with these questions. The next section introduces a broad framework for analysing industrial policy. The third section considers the experience of other Asia-Pacific economies faced with policy choices similar to those of Hong Kong. The final section argues that Hong Kong's industrial policy should now seek a new direction, and provides some broad guidelines for future policy.

The Rationale for an Industrial Policy

Simply put, the theoretical rationale for industrial policy is market failure. Industrial policy emerged as a category of economic policy during the period of postwar recovery in Western European countries. These countries were the first to recognize that the market, when left to its own devices, does not necessarily produce the best allocation of resources among sectors of the economy, or the most rapid growth of industry.

Subsequent debates have produced two broad schools of thought on industrial policy: the 'neoclassical' and the 'structuralist' schools. While both schools agree that government intervention is called for where there is market failure, there is disagreement about the likely extent of market failure and therefore the appropriate degree of intervention.

According to the neoclassical school, government intervention should be relatively light and limited to a few selected cases so that the allocation decisions of the private sector are not substantially affected. 'Picking winners' by the government, that is the identification of industries with growth potential, should be avoided, because on top of market failure, there could be 'government failure'. The industrial policy of Hong Kong largely follows the neoclassical line of thought; the traditional role of the Hong Kong government in industrial development has been to support and reinforce market signals. The government has never attempted to nourish strategic industries, although a group of 'priority industries' has been identified in the recent years.

The structuralists argue that given market failure, the government should attempt to influence the pattern of industrialization. The government, which is assumed to be more powerful and better informed than the private sector, should select and encourage new industries that have the potential for long-run, self-sustained growth. In the developing countries where the private sector remains weak, government's role in industrial development should be assertive, forceful, and comprehensive. The industrial policy of Taiwan, Singapore, and South Korea, has so far followed the structuralist line to varying degrees.

Market Failure and Industrial Policy

The economist Richard Caves, one of the pioneers on the theory of industrial policy, suggests three basic circumstances when the government might apply corrective measures. The first is related to the production of industrial knowledge and new technology. The second arises when an economy has a monopoly over an export, and the third where the market does not work well to reallocate resources, for example, where wages are inflexible.

The second and the third types of market failure identified by Caves have not been present in Hong Kong to any significant degree. Hong Kong firms and industries are not able to act as international oligopolies, nor is the Hong Kong economy slow to adjust to changing situations. Any argument that present-day Hong Kong needs increasingly active government participation in industrialization must be based on the fact that the economy has, since 1979, moved into a new phase of industrial production, the production of more sophisticated, high-technology products. The key issue is the role of the government in supporting technological change.

If there is to be adequate investment in innovative activities, the producer of new knowledge, having incurred the costs and taken the risks, should be able to earn a return from the use of the innovation equal to the benefits it yields. But full appropriation of benefits by a producer of knowledge is not in fact desirable from a social point of view, nor is it generally possible.

Full appropriation is not *desirable* because it implies monopoly control of new ideas. The return on knowledge (or the process or product embodying it) will be extracted from the public by the sale of goods at a price higher than their cost, even including the costs of development. But commercially valuable knowledge is like any other useful information. Once it is available, society can only benefit if more people make productive use of it.

Full appropriation is not usually *feasible* because, over time, new ideas become accessible to all the potential users. As the technology diffuses, other firms begin to capture part of the benefits yielded by the invention, either directly by using the new technology, or indirectly because it reduces the cost of their inputs.

Without public support, investors tend to underinvest in innovative activities because as the technology diffuses, the social benefit from innovative investment becomes greater than its private benefit.

If Hong Kong seeks to become a generator of new technologies, two features of the production and use of new ideas will have to be taken into account. Firstly, large scale is necessary to develop new technology. Since Hong Kong firms are, by international standards, small, a collective, government-led effort may be necessary to succeed. Secondly, the risks involved in research and development are high. This is a powerful additional constraint on private activity, and an additional factor suggesting that government support will be required. The closer Hong Kong approaches the existing international technology frontier, the more important industrial policy will be to economic growth and development.

The Regional Context

Since Hong Kong is highly internationalized and functions as an integral part of the Asia–Pacific region, discussion of the development of its industrial policy must be placed in the regional context and must be viewed from the regional perspective. In fact, the new dynamism of regional growth, a dynamism based on technological development, serves as the main motive for the planners to work to rethink Hong Kong's industrial policy.

'Regionalization' and 'Asianization' are the new growth factors in the Asia–Pacific area. Production inputs in Asia now flow more freely than ever before across national borders. Asia is becoming increasingly a single economy. This trend has been intensified by changing government policy in Asia in support of economic liberalization.

As the region becomes a huge production base, sharing

among member economies technology, capital, and man-power, production capacity is enhanced, economies of scale in production are easier to achieve, and the pace of industrial upgrading becomes quicker. 'Regionalization' and 'Asianization' mean that, in the future, Asia will be a growth hub of the global economy and a major recipient of overseas capital. Whether Hong Kong is able to exploit these new opportun-ities as they emerge, and reap fully the benefits deriving from multinational activities, depends critically on the economy's knowledge-generating and assimilating capacity.

Since the 1970s, a new pattern of the sub-regional division of labour has developed in the Asia–Pacific area. The ASEAN countries and China are catching up with the Asian Newly Industrialized Economies (ANIEs) in labour-intensive manu-factures, while the ANIEs are catching up with Japan in tech-nology and knowledge-intensive products.

This crude ordering of labour-intensive to knowledge-intensive economies can be understood better when it is recog-nized that production processes involve a finer and finer international division of labour, with a large share of interna-tional trade made up of parts and components. Detailed prod-uct specifications have to be met by producers of these components to ensure the quality of the final product. The regional division of labour implies a regional division of knowledge. Product specialization has given rise to knowl-edge specialization.

Older strategies for technological development have ceased to be useful. Technological borrowing by unpacking a com-plex good embodying a more advanced technology and then reconstructing simplified local versions has become increas-ingly difficult. Nor can countries expect to develop techno-logical sophistication simply through foreign investment. Innovation and invention depend on a well-developed tech-nology infrastructure — an abundant supply of scientists, a highly educated work force, entrepreneurs equipped to take advantage of new methods, financial resources, and not least a strong technology policy. As a result, innovation will be-come concentrated increasingly in a few privileged econo-mies in East and South-East Asia. The intra-regional technology gap will widen.

How can the technology gap with the other ANIEs be nar-rowed? How can the productivity of Hong Kong industry be

increased? Given the problems associated with private production of new technologies, it is unlikely that a purely non-
interventionist strategy will be adequate.

Government Failure

Any demand for enhanced government activity has to face
the problem that the identification of market failure capable
of solution by appropriate government policy does not necessarily imply that any particular government will in fact
improve economic performance. 'Government failure' may
be as much of a problem as market failure. Industrial policy
is never a purely economic instrument. The analysis of industrial policy should always include the political environment
within which it is made. Political actors, serving their own
interests rather than overall welfare, often manipulate industrial policy to attain economic objectives. For example, a
government which depends on the support of landlords or
businessmen to strengthen its political status may manipulate the land and business tax systems in such a way that the
laws coincide with the interests of its supporters. Administration of policies may also be weak and incompetent, or dominated by the interests of administrators. However, the possibility
of government failure argues for caution, not for inaction.

The difficulty then is to formulate appropriate industrial-
policy initiatives in an environment where the market is likely
to provide inadequate incentives for the development of new
technologies and innovation, but where the risk of making
costly mistakes with public money is also high. Hong Kong
is not alone in facing this challenge and the experience of
other regional economies is therefore relevant.

The Asia–Pacific Experience with
Industrial Policy

Industrial policy in the Asia–Pacific region can be classified
into two different categories: (1) 'diffusion oriented' industrial policy, and (2) 'mission-oriented' industrial policy. While
the industrial policy of some economies falls neatly and dis-
tinctly into one category — Hong Kong's diffusion-oriented

policies for example — other industrial policy approaches share the characteristics of both.

Under mission-oriented industrialization, the government pursues a 'mission' and intervenes actively to attain a well defined set of goals. Under diffusion-oriented industrialization, the government's role is to provide the infrastructure to enhance production and technological diffusion. It aims to facilitate change rather than to direct it.

Japan has provided regional economies with the clearest example of an apparently successful, mission-oriented industrial policy. Ministry of Trade and Industry (MITI) has played an important role in Japan's industrial policy. Via MITI, the Japanese government has provided strong leadership with regard to the direction of industrialization. MITI picked the winners and then backed them up with a comprehensive package of support which included generous tax incentives and subsidies. Above all, the Japanese government combined trade policy with industrial policy. Japanese infant industries were not generally exposed to foreign competition until they were able to survive. Unfortunately, from the consumer-welfare perspective, trade measures such as import tariffs and export quotas reduce consumer choices, increase product prices, and lower quality.

The Japanese 'lesson' has been learned most obviously by South Korea, where the direction of industrial development can be described as determined from 'above'. Among the four ANIEs, industrial policy in South Korea is the most elaborate, comprehensive, forceful, and interventionist. Planners have made extensive and coercive use of a wide range of incentives. Large business conglomerates have been protected by the government to push up investment levels and growth rates. In addition to incentives and subsidies, tariffs and quotas have been used extensively. It was not until the middle of the 1980s that the Korean government attempted to pursue trade liberalization. Not surprisingly in the Korean case, 'government failure' was not rare. In particular, after 1977 when the Korean government implemented drastic measures to promote capital- and skill-intensive developments, many costly mistakes were made by the central authority.

The industrial policy of Taiwan has been more interventionist than that of Hong Kong. Initially, the Taiwan government's aim was to formulate a free-trade and free-market regime. In the 1960s and 1970s, investment decisions were left to the private sector. Since the 1980s, slower economic growth and rising labour costs suggested that manufacturing in Taiwan required upgrading. Consequently, in order to attract the establishment of higher-skill and higher-technology industries, the Taiwanese government began to provide financial incentives. These incentives included low-interest loans and tax holidays. More neutral measures were also widely used including the setting up of the Hsinchu Science Park and various industrial estates, and the signing of technology cooperation contracts with foreign governments.

In the event, the pioneer investments attracted to Taiwan were MacDonald's and Kentucky Fried Chicken rather than the desired knowledge-intensive petrochemical and biotechnology plants. This suggests that the Taiwanese government continued a tradition of letting business seek out opportunities. Nevertheless, tariffs (fortunately, not quotas, an instrument which is harmful to consumer welfare) are still used to meet industrial objectives.

Singapore's experience with industrial policy is arguably the most relevant to Hong Kong. Like Hong Kong, Singapore has maintained free trade to a large extent and encourages a highly competitive domestic economy. Although foreign direct investment has been warmly welcomed, no preferential treatment has been given to foreign investors. But, like South Korea, the development of Singapore's private sector has been kept under strict control by the government. Via fiscal and financial incentives, the government has largely steered the direction of research and development.

In Singapore, as in South Korea, picking winners seems to have been easier before the late 1970s when the economy's comparative advantage obviously lay with labour-intensive products. In the 1980s, as Singapore's comparative advantage shifted more towards skill- and capital-intensive products, the government has found it more difficult to select priority sectors from among a large group of infant industries all requiring huge investments in technology and capital. As a result, the Singapore government has also made costly mistakes. In fact, the 1985 economic recession of Singapore resulted in part from the National Wage Council's high-wage policy. This policy, implemented in 1979, was an attempt to raise wage levels artificially to discourage low-skill, labour-intensive activities.

In an important recent paper, Alwyn Young has shown that over the past twenty years Singapore's economic growth has depended on capital accumulation. It has enjoyed very little increase in 'total factor productivity', normally the result of technological progress. Young suggests that Singapore's active industrial policy has encouraged shifting from one product to another too rapidly. Only relatively long experience in an industry can lead to the productivity improvement that comes with 'learning by doing'.

These frequent examples of 'government failure' have significant policy implications. As an economy enters the technology phase of industrial production, it is true that its government should play a more active role to bring research activities up to a socially optimal level. However, this is also the time when the number of options increases. As a result, the chance that the government will pick losers, not winners, also rises. In addition, as the overhead cost of research activities becomes more substantial, the risk, and the cost of research failure, a cost now borne more by the government rather than by the private sector, also becomes higher. Simply put, as knowledge-generating capacity becomes more crucial to industrial success, both the possibility and the cost of 'government failure' is larger.

The Future Direction of Hong Kong's Industrial Policy

In the past two decades, public policy in Hong Kong relating to industrial development has been basically educational, infrastructural, and service oriented. The government has deliberately avoided resorting to fiscal and financial incentives, such as tax holidays and subsidies. It was not until the early 1990s that the government introduced modest financial incentives — such as the Technology Loan Fund (1989–90), the Applied Technology Matching Grant (1992), and the New Technology Training Scheme (1992) — to achieve economic targets.

Despite recent initiatives, the industrial policy of Hong Kong has been the most passive and market-oriented in the Asia–Pacific region. Tables 2.1 and 2.2 show government expenditure on industrial research and development (R&D) and on

Table 2.1 Government Expenditure on Industrial Research and Development (R&D) in Hong Kong, Singapore, Taiwan, South Korea, and Japan, 1989/90

Industralized Countries in Asia Pacific	Year 1989/90 (as percentage of total government expenditure)	Year 1989/90 (as percentage of GNP or GDP)**
Japan*	0.746	0.1150
Hong Kong	0.034	0.0055
Singapore	0.637	0.1973
Taiwan	0.588	0.1559
South Korea*	1.121	0.2300

Sources: Hong Kong Government Census and Statistics Department, *Estimates for Revenue, Funds, Capital Account Commitments, Staff Establishments and Pay Scales 1990*, Government Printer, 1991.
Singapore Government Ministry of Finance, *Singapore Budget for the Financial Year 1989–90*, 1991.
Republic of China National Science Council, *Indicators of Science and Technology 1989 and 1990*, 1990 and 1991.
The Bank of Korea, *Monthly Statistical Bulletin*, April 1993.
The Japan Economic Journal: Nihon Keizai Shimbun, Inc., *Japan Economic Almanac 1989 and 1990*, 1989 and 1990.

Notes: * Due to data constraints, the figures for Japan and South Korea denote the relative shares of government expenditure on R&D to promote science and technology rather than on industrial R&D.
   ** As the percentage of total GDP for Hong Kong and as the percentage of total GNP for South Korea, Singapore, Taiwan, and Japan.

education in Japan and the four ANIEs. Hong Kong shows much lower levels of public expenditure on industrial R&D relative to her Asian counterparts, but a relatively high level of government expenditure on education.

There is then a strong case for the Hong Kong government to take a larger role in the support of the technological development of local industry. Without such support it is clear that the movement to higher value-added processes will be slow, and without more support there is a real danger that our industries will fall behind other economies in the region.

Table 2.2 Government Expenditure on Education in Hong Kong, Singapore, Taiwan, South Korea, and Japan, 1990/1

Industrialized Countries in Asia Pacific	Year 1990/1 (as percentage of total government expenditure)	Year 1990/1 (as percentage of GNP or GDP)**
Japan*	8.5	1.5
Hong Kong	15.0	2.4
Singapore	13.3	3.3
Taiwan	12.8	2.5
South Korea*	18.5	2.7

Sources: Hong Kong Government, *The Hong Kong Yearbook 1991*, Hong Kong, Government Printer, 1991.
Singapore Government Ministry of Communications and Information, *The Singapore Yearbook 1991*, Singapore, Singapore National Printers Ltd., 1991.
Republic of China Ministry of Education, *Education Statistics of the Republic of China 1990*, Republic of China, 1991. Numbers 4 and 5 of Table 2.

Notes: ** As the percentage of total GDP for Hong Kong and as the percentage of total GNP for South Korea, Singapore, Taiwan, and Japan.

The analysis suggests, however, that this support need not be targeted to specific firms or sectors. The problem is to create an 'infrastructure' that facilitates the adoption and adaptation of technologies that are developing world-wide. The elements of that infrastructure are a critical mass of technical workers, technically sophisticated managers capable of recognizing and using new technology, and the availability of financial resources — risk capital — that can be invested in new projects. Since the private venture-capital market that might shoulder part of the inventor's risk is underdeveloped in Hong Kong, the government is the only probable source of high-risk capital. Through the government, the public can share the risk of inventions that will ultimately benefit them.

The shape of such a policy will have to take into account the important changes now taking place in Hong Kong's manufacturing industry, notably the new division of labour between Hong Kong itself and the manufacturing base emerging in southern China. A survey by the Centre for Asian Studies at the University of Hong Kong in the summer of 1993 has made clear the significance of this development. Three points emerged from this survey that help indicate a way forward.

Deindustrialization of the Manufacturing Sector

Surprisingly, the management of *all* the manufacturing firms interviewed, both the larger and the smaller ones, claimed that their companies have no manufacturing activities at all in Hong Kong. All manufacturing activities have been relocated to China to minimize material and labour costs and to internalize the locational advantages of China by making direct investments there. The Hong Kong bases of these companies are assuming non-manufacturing, or manufacturing-related, roles, which include one or more of the following activities: material sourcing, quality control, marketing, technology acquisition and consultation, production planning, and product and mould designing. The manager of a textile firm in Hong Kong emphasized that the future focus would be on finishing services such as bleaching, dyeing, stencilling, and printing.

There is then an opening for the Hong Kong government to accelerate and support the development of these manufacturing-related activities. For example, Hong Kong industrialists have been striving hard to develop original product designs and to develop brand names with an international presence, such as Unimax and Playwell enjoy in the toy business. Government support is required to nourish, educate, and provide opportunities for creative young designers and marketing people capable of giving local products a global edge.

The Hong Kong government is now making efforts to encourage originality in product design. Hong Kong Polytechnic University offers degree training in product design and development. The Hong Kong Industrial Technology Centre Corporation (HKITCC) provides support services to high-technology industries such as updating design technology for manufacturers. To encourage a spirit of creativity, the Federation of Hong Kong Industries and the Chinese Manufacturers' Association have, in the past few years, organized design competitions for consumer products and for machinery and equipment.

Problems in the area of product design are not principally a matter of training and infrastructure. They are rather a problem of outreach to industry, especially to small- and medium-scale enterprises (SMEs). The government-industry-university link in design and development needs to be strengthened. Promotion of the existing facilities, placement of design graduates in appropriate firms, and forums and conventions that bring together designers and manufacturers to exchange ideas and information and to share new opportunities would all be useful.

Hong Kong is the only newly industrialized economy in Asia which does not use government subsidies to promote product design. As the cost and risk of designing and developing a new product becomes higher, the government should consider providing financial and/or fiscal incentives to firms which are expanding their design and application departments.

Human Capital and Corporate Success

The management of all the manufacturing firms interviewed stated that in recent years, acquiring skilled workers and promoting research activity has become a major part of corporate strategy. The largest firms have research centres and training centres in Hong Kong, China, or both. The usual practice is to transfer managers, supervisors, technicians, and engineers from the parent company to the subsidiary to provide on-the-job training to PRC employees, or to operate training centres in China. Extensive training, targeted at both Hong Kong and PRC staff, is done in Hong Kong.

Industrial policy used to enhance the skills base of Hong Kong firms must also seek to enhance that of their subsidiaries located in China, or in other parts of the region. A more productive subsidiary means a better product, an enhanced reputation, and a higher profit margin for the parent company. Above all, if 'technology deepening' occurs in China, so that the Chinese subsidiary performs more skill- and technology-intensive production processes, the pace of industrial restructuring and upgrading can be increased in Hong Kong.

The Hong Kong government already pays considerable attention to education and training. Unfortunately, government efforts to promote industrial training are mainly directed to training institutions, not to firms. This prevents firms from making full use of the resources available. A reorganization of programmes and the redirection of expenditures is required.

The government might consider establishing industry-specific training centres to meet the needs of individual industries. In addition, the government might consider introducing a Manufacturing Training Award Scheme to give recognition to firms which have achieved outstanding achievements in employee training.

Research indicates that small- and medium-sized firms in Hong Kong cannot compete with larger companies in training activities or in marketing and technology acquisition. This suggests that government resources need to be redirected. If financial assistance is required, the government might consider following the practice in Singapore by inviting banks and financial institutions to participate in its investments in smaller firms on a risk-sharing basis.

Networking in Hong Kong

From our interviews, we concluded that 'networking' will continue to be a major element in plans for corporate expansion, particularly where they involve an outward flow of direct investment from Hong Kong.

The South China Economic Zone, especially the Hong Kong–Guangdong area, will be the major location for this network formation. Networking is becoming an essential aspect of business life as the manufacturing process evolves. Typically, Hong Kong firms provide materials for their subsidiaries in China (or in other parts of the region) for further processing of parts and components. When orders are too large for the subsidiary to handle, it may subcontract the work to other local firms in the host country. The final assembly of parts and components is done either in Hong Kong or in the subsidiary. The major aim of networking is to enhance vertical integration and self-sufficiency. Network formation increases production efficiency, makes planning feasible, and hedges the producer against external shocks that disturb the production schedule.

Hitherto, the Hong Kong government has played only a low-key role in support of business networking. To promote inward investment, the Hong Kong Industry Department set up a one-stop information unit in 1983 to provide all-round assistance to investors from overseas. Industrial promotion units were set up in six major international cities to safeguard and advance Hong Kong's economic, commercial, and political interests overseas and to maintain close liaison with the business sectors of these cities. Through a network of thirty-seven branches in twenty-six countries, the Hong Kong Trade Development Council promotes Hong Kong products overseas and generates international awareness of the business opportunities available in Hong Kong.

Business networking usually involves the outflow of investment, but so far, our government has done very little to help local businessmen to network overseas. Financial incentives such as low interest loans could be used to encourage local manufacturers to integrate their production internationally. In addition, a service package which includes the speedy provision of market and legal information on the host country and on assistance in finding business partners and office space could be offered to local businessmen to help them get established on foreign soil.

This chapter has called for rethinking the future direction of Hong Kong's industrial policy.

As an economy enters the high-technology phase of industrial production, its government should play a more active role to bring research and development up to a socially optimal level. One of the reasons why Hong Kong has been slow to produce high-end products is that, unlike Singapore, Taiwan, and South Korea, Hong Kong provides no subsidies to help in the development of new products. If the manufacturing sector is to remain a critical component of the Hong Kong economy, incentives such as subsidies for research and development and tax holidays to hedge against initial business losses will be essential.

The question is, can the government detect market signals better than the private sector? After all, 'laissez-faire liberalism' has brought miraculous economic success to Hong Kong in the past twenty years, so why we do need to change?

There are a number of reasons why a government may be better equipped and more effective in detecting market signals and responding to them compared with the private sector. Firstly, a government has the resources necessary to examine the complex and dynamic world situation and its impacts on local economic development. Secondly, inter-governmental exchanges allow access to first-hand information regarding global markets and policy changes that affect them. Thirdly, a government is able to plan and to systematically implement change, making the pace of economic restructuring quicker and the fruits of such restructuring easier to reap. Fourthly, the distribution of economic gains to emerging industries, the 'winners', can be faster with government support than when these gains are distributed by the market. If the pay-off period is shorter, reinvestment along the right track is encouraged.

This is not to say that a highly interventionist industrial policy is appropriate to the economic context of Hong Kong. Hong Kong must still find the industrial policy direction that best suits the economy's unique development history, geographical site, and factor endowment.

Hong Kong has experienced a high rate of technological progress in the past twenty years. The hands-off policy of her government has allowed entrepreneurs and investors to enjoy a maximum degree of flexibility. Decisions of local entrepreneurs have not been disrupted as they were in Singapore. Skills were nourished and new products were developed at the appropriate time. We have no evidence to show that in Hong Kong the response to market signals is too slow. There are unexploited niches in the production of Hong Kong's traditional products.

Industrial policy can operate at four levels: (1) the government can substitute itself for the market; (2) the government can steer the market; (3) the government can detect, facilitate, and support market signals; and (4) the government can refuse to intervene in the market. How far up this ladder should Hong Kong shift its industrial policy? Given Hong Kong's unique economic development history, her traditional 'laissez-faire liberalism' does not need to be changed fundamentally. The government should not intervene aggressively to steer the market, but should shape its policy of industrial support to coincide as much as possible with market signals.

3. Reforming Hong Kong's Fiscal System

Tang Shu-hung

H60
E62

The Hong Kong government has long pursued a conservative fiscal policy, a policy consistent with its positive non-interventionism in managing the economy. With a political system free from any electoral influence on policy formulation, at least up to the 1991 partial direct election of the Legislative Council, and given the instructions of the Colonial Regulations to remain financially viable, the main objective of fiscal policy remains to maintain the financial stability of the Hong Kong government. The huge fiscal reserve accumulated over the past forty years clearly demonstrates that this objective has been firmly adhered to.

Recent developments in Hong Kong's socio-political-economic system inevitably exert an influence on the formulation of fiscal policy and on the performance of the fiscal system. These developments include: the process of gradual democratization of the Hong Kong political system which started in 1985; demands for greater fairness and enhanced social programmes in an increasingly rich and aging community; restructuring towards a more service-oriented economy; the impact of the Basic Law of the Hong Kong Special Administrative Region which was passed in April 1990 in Beijing, which contains articles on budgetary principles; and the impact of the Memorandum of Understanding on Hong Kong's New Airport and Related Matters (MOU) signed in July 1991 by the governments of the United Kingdom and the People's Republic of China, which outlines financial commitments that must be honoured by the Hong Kong government.

Some of these developments create a need for the government to increase public spending on social and economic programmes, and to reform the tax system to enhance social and economic equity. This implies that greater fiscal flexibility, if not active fiscal policy, will be required. Unfortunately, the Basic Law and the MOU stipulate an even more conservative and restrictive approach in fiscal management. This chapter is concerned with the policy problem that is emerging as the requirement for greater fiscal flexibility runs up against the government's conventional approach to the budget, and the rigidity of the constitutional arrangements that have been put in place.

Fiscal Philosophy and Budgetary Guidelines

The essentially bureaucratic control of Hong Kong's fiscal policy has a long history. The fiscal principle imposed on the Colony was self-support and a balanced budget, so that there was no need for the exchequer of the United Kingdom to subsidize the Colony.

In 1870, the Hong Kong government was released from treasury control and was given a greater degree of autonomy over its own finances and in 1958, the government was granted quasi-full financial autonomy. But increasing financial autonomy has not meant relaxing prudential financial management.

Hong Kong has never experimented with 'Keynesian' deficit budget financing to manage aggregate demand, 'fine-tuning' the economy to reduce the amplitude of cyclical fluctuations. Even during recession periods, contrary to the prescriptions of anti-cyclical fiscal policy, budget deficits have been used as an opportunity to raise tax rates, or to levy new taxes.

Successive Hong Kong financial secretaries have emphasized the value of not pursuing systematic or continuous deficit financing. Although there have been twenty-three deficit budgets since 1946/7, there were only seven financial years in which actual deficits were realized. The government has issued only HK$1.2 billion in public bonds to finance its budget deficits.

The sharp contrast between actual and estimated budgets suggests that the government has pursued a budgeting strategy of deliberately overestimating expenditure and underestimating revenues. Underspending in some years has been as high as 10 per cent of budget estimates.

Deficit budgets have usually resulted from increases in proposed expenditure on social and economic services essential for development. The 1993/4 deficit budget, for example, proposed the use of fiscal reserves to assist in financing the new airport. Actual budget deficits have also resulted from world economic recessions, such as that in 1982, that exert a detrimental effect on taxation revenues. In 1982/3 the planned surplus turned out to be a huge deficit, the largest in Hong Kong's history. Despite occasional deficits, by 1995, the government had accumulated almost HK$150 billion of fiscal revenues, 86 per cent of total public expenditure.

At the operational level, successive financial secretaries have developed and refined budgetary guidelines. These budgetary guidelines are a special feature of the Hong Kong fiscal regime.

In the 1970s, five budgetary guideline ratios were included in the medium-range forecast. Table 3.1 provides additional details of the evolution of these guideline ratios. The five guideline ratios aimed to define sufficiency of recurrent revenues. For example, recurrent revenues should at least cover a certain proportion of total expenditure, and the surplus in the recurrent account should at least reach a minimum proportion of non-recurrent (i.e. capital) expenditure.

In 1986/7, Financial Secretary Piers Jacobs simplified these five budgetary guideline ratios by condensing them to only one ratio — that the surplus in the recurrent account must at least be able to pay for half of non-recurrent expenditure (see the last column of Table 3.1). The objective of this guideline is to limit the deficit, if any, to not more than half of non-recurrent expenditure.

Table 3.2 shows the size of the public sector in Hong Kong (1970–97). The government has argued that the size of the public sector should not be greater than 20 per cent of gross domestic product (GDP). It can be seen from the table that the public sector share of GDP peaked in 1982/3 at over 18.5 per cent. While it is expected to reach close to 20 per cent in the period to 1997, it will not exceed the 20 per cent psychological ceiling. The guideline ratio on the growth of real total public expenditure was first set at a specific percentage, but was amended in 1986/7 to a real growth rate not exceeding the trend assumption growth rate in GDP.

It is interesting to note that the budgetary guideline ratio given in Table 3.1 does not rule out the possibility of a deficit budget, but a budgetary guideline on total cash-flow surplus/deficit was proposed in 1986/7. The guideline emphasizes obtaining an annual cash-flow surplus (from 1986/7 to 1992/3) in order to maintain the real value of the total balance of the General Revenue Account and the Funds (i.e. fiscal reserves).

Table 3.1 Hong Kong: Budgetary Guideline Ratios

Guideline Ratios		Before 1975/6	1975/6–1981/2	1982/3–1985/6	1986/7–Present
(1) Recurrent Revenues Total Expenditure	At Least	—	88%	77%	—
(2) Recurrent Expenditure Recurrent Revenues	Not More Than	70%	80%	85%	—
(3) Surplus in Recurrent Account Non-recurrent Expenditure	At Least	75%	60%	33%	50%
(4) Recurrent Expenditure Total Expenditure	Not More Than	—	70%	65%	—
(5) Non-recurrent Revenues Non-recurrent Expenditure	At Least	25%	20%	20%	—

Sources: S. H. Tang, *Issues of Public Finance in Hong Kong* (in Chinese), Wide Angle Press, Hong Kong, 1988, p. 6. *Budget*, Hong Kong, various issues.

Table 3.2 Size of the Public Sector in Hong Kong

Financial Year	Size of the Public Sector	Financial Year	Size of the Public Sector
1961/2	13.8%	1980/1	15.6%
1962/3	13.7%	1981/2	17.2%
1963/4	13.3%	1982/3	18.5%
1964/5	12.9%	1983/4	18.1%
1965/6	13.2%	1984/5	15.5%
1966/7	13.1%	1985/6	16.0%
1967/8	12.0%	1986/7	15.3%
1968/9	11.7%	1987/8	13.9%
1969/70	10.9%	1988/9	14.2%
1970/1	10.9%	1989/90	15.6%
1971/2	11.1%	1990/1	16.3%
1972/3	12.1%	1991/2	16.2%
1973/4	12.3%	1992/3	15.8%
1974/5	14.3%	1993/4	17.3%
1975/6	13.4%	1994/5*	16.8%
1976/7	11.7%	1995/6**	17.6%
1977/8	12.6%	1996/7+	17.6%
1978/9	14.2%	1997/8+	17.8%
1979/80	14.0%	1998/9+	17.8%

Sources: *Budget*, Hong Kong, various issues, and *Estimates of Gross Domestic Product: 1961 to 1994*, March 1995.

Notes: The size of the public sector has been scaled down due to the upward revision of the GDP in August 1994 to take into account the restructuring of the economy. In the latest issue of *Estimates of Gross Domestic Product* published in March 1995, the estimates of the 1961 to 1965 GDP were published for the first time. Except for the 1995/6 budget estimate and the Medium Range Forecast projected values, all other figures of the size of the public sector are calculated from the actual values of total public expenditure and GDP.

* Revised estimate.
** Budget estimate.
+ Forecast value.

When the financial secretary adopted new budgetary guideline ratios in 1986/7, no guideline ratio on fiscal reserves was included. However, calculations by the author indicate the operation of an implicit guideline. Table 3.3 shows the level of fiscal reserves since 1986/7.

In his maiden budget speech presented in March 1992, Financial Secretary Hamish Macleod defined a reasonable level of fiscal reserves as the amount necessary to meet the government's commitments under the MOU, while maintaining a reasonable cushion against the contingencies of the forecast period. Macleod explained further that 'it is plainly unnecessary to build up our reserves above the level which prudent judgement and past experience justify'. This is in conformity with the guideline on total cash-flow surplus/deficit which states that the government aims to maintain adequate reserves in the long term.

Taxes

Hong Kong has a simple tax system, a system that has not changed much since the 1950s. There are only four kinds of direct taxes: profits tax, salaries tax, property tax, and estates tax. The interest tax was abolished in 1989, and capital gains are not taxed. There are very few indirect taxes in Hong Kong. They include: excise duties, general rates and internal revenue (i.e. bets and sweeps taxes, hotel accommodation tax, entertainment tax, tunnel tax, airport passenger departure tax), motor vehicle taxes, and franchises and concessions. No general broad-based consumption tax is levied.

Sir Philip Haddon-Cave stipulated the following six objectives of the Hong Kong tax system in the 1978/9 budget:

1. The tax system should help to generate sufficient recurrent revenue to finance a major part of total public expenditure and to maintain government's fiscal reserves at a satisfactory level.
2. The tax system should be as neutral as possible as regards the internal cost/price structure and investment decisions.
3. The laws governing the tax system should be adapted from time to time to make them consistent with changing commercial practices.

Table 3.3 Hong Kong — The Level of Fiscal Reserves, HK$ million (1986/7 to 1998/9)

Financial Year	Fiscal Reserves at the Beginning of the Financial Year — Budget Estimate (1)	Fiscal Reserves at the End of the Financial Year — Budget Projection (2)	Total Government Expenditure at the Beginning of the Financial Year — Budget Estimate (3)	(1) (3) (%)	(2) (3) (%)
1986/7	25,833	26,293	42,990	60.1%	61.2%
1987/8	32,020	34,420	48,490	66.0%	71.0%
1988/9	40,510	45,970	55,540	72.9%	82.8%
1989/90	59,640	71,110	69,070	86.3%	103.0%
1990/1	70,800	71,520	90,980	77.8%	78.6%
1991/2	72,730	74,030	101,280	71.8%	73.1%
1992/3	99,355	91,805	115,100	86.3%	79.8%
1993/4	119,590	116,230	132,460	90.3%	87.7%
1994/5	136,130	143,790	146,020	93.2%	98.5%
1995/6	147,930	145,310	169,740	87.2%	85.6%
1996/7*	145,310	151,260	190,200	76.4%	79.5%
1997/8*	151,260	184,580	221,480	68.3%	83.3%
		(327,490)**			
1998/9*	327,490**	360,690**	257,220	127.3%	147.9%
					140.2%

Source: Calculated from Budget, Hong Kong, various issues.
Notes: * The Medium Range Forecast period of the 1995/6 Budget.
      ** Including Land Fund.

4. Each and every levy, be it direct or indirect, should be simple and easy (and, therefore, inexpensive) to administer and not encourage evasion, for a low and narrowly based tax system cannot afford to finance costly overheads.
5. The tax system should be equitable between different classes of taxpayers or potential taxpayers and between different income groups (and this means, *inter alia*, setting relatively high thresholds for personal taxation and generally ensuring that the system rests as lightly as possible on the disposable incomes of those at the lower end of the income spectrum, or leaves them virtually untouched).
6. Exceptionally, the tax system must be capable of being used to achieve non-fiscal objectives when necessary.

In other words, revenue productivity, neutrality, adaptability, simplicity, and equity are the requirements of the Hong Kong tax system, with revenue productivity assuming the priority position. Though the most important objective of the tax system is to generate sufficient recurrent revenues, Hong Kong does not impose high taxes. The current profits tax rate is 16.5 per cent, the lowest among all industrialized and newly industrialized economies. The standard tax rate is even lower at 15 per cent. These two rates have never reached the 20 per cent level since the inception of the Inland Revenue Ordinance in 1947/8.

Taxes and Income Distribution

One of the possible objectives of fiscal policy is to obtain a more equitable income distribution. This has never been attempted in Hong Kong. Successive financial secretaries have asserted that the Hong Kong tax system is not to be used to redistribute income, because this is not consistent with a simple tax system or low tax rates. Only the salaries tax has a progressive marginal rate schedule and, under the standard tax rate clause, even the salaries tax becomes proportional for middle- and higher-income groups.

By taxing income at a low rate, and exempting capital gains from taxation, the Hong Kong tax system favours the accumulation of wealth, which worsens income disparity. Census and by-census data since 1971 show that overall income disparity has increased over the past two decades. Indeed the distribution of household income depicts an alarming situation. The 1991 population census showed that compared with 1981, only the top 20 per cent of households experienced an improving share of overall income, while the bottom 80 per cent suffered losses of income share.

Tax Reform

In the 1980s, nearly all major industrialized countries and many developing countries set up committees or commissions to review comprehensively their respective tax systems to make them more responsive to social and economic needs. Some members of the Hong Kong Legislative Council have proposed that the government conduct a similarly comprehensive review of the Hong Kong tax system. But the business community and the government do not favour the idea. In February 1992, just two weeks before the 1992/3 budget speech, the government manoeuvred the support of unofficial legislative councillors having business interests to defeat a motion 'urging the government to set up a committee, with members representing a wide cross-section of the community to conduct a comprehensive review of the taxation system in Hong Kong'. Without a comprehensive review of the existing tax system, it will be impossible to introduce any radical reform.

Previously, the government has floated proposals to increase the role of indirect taxes, arguing that placing a greater burden on indirect taxation will increase the revenue productivity and stability of the tax system. A proposal was included in the 1988/9 budget to consider the introduction of a wholesale sales tax. This is a broad-based consumption tax. If it were to be introduced, it would raise the contribution from indirect taxes to 45 per cent of the total tax revenues in Hong Kong. Because of strong objections from political parties and the Legislative Council, this reform proposal has been shelved temporarily. If the wholesale sales tax were introduced, it would worsen the already high degree of income disparity.

Other recent moves will have the same effect. Beginning in 1989, the government has been pursuing a new public-sector pricing policy aiming to reduce the public subsidy of social services by charging higher prices to recoup fully or partially the cost of these services. Many social welfare services that were previously a citizen's entitlement will gradually become means-tested. The purpose of the new policy on public-sector pricing is to control the growth of public expenditure and to maintain the financial stability of the government. Since social services mainly affect the livelihood of ordinary and lower-income groups, the new policy will achieve financial stability at the cost of greater income disparity.

Paradoxically, as the economy becomes more sophisticated and developed and as Hong Kong becomes more open and democratic, the Hong Kong government has chosen to reject any genuine tax reform exercise and to emphasize the role of indirect taxation and public-sector pricing in achieving financial stability. This approach is completely different from that demanded by the general public.

Revenue and Expenditure

It may seem surprising that a simple tax regime with low rates can generate sufficient revenue to maintain the solid financial position of the government, while other countries suffer from huge budgetary deficits even with high tax rates and prolific tax impositions. The Laffer-curve proposition that the disincentive effect of higher taxes shrinks the tax base because of a resulting lower level of economic activity can be viewed as one of the underlying reasons for Hong Kong's success with its low tax rate policy. But this point should not be over-emphasized. There are other contributing factors which should not be overlooked.

Firstly, the government contains the growth of public expenditure and the size of the public sector. Secondly, the tax-subsidy system is insensitive to economic fluctuations. The government has not established unemployment insurance and the tax system lacks progressivity. Thirdly, the Hong Kong government spells out clearly that the tax system is not used to redistribute income. It is the common view, both of the business community and the government, that the profits tax rate should not be above a 20 per cent maximum. Fourthly, the economy enjoyed a long period of high growth with full employment.

Social Welfare

Formulating an appropriate and affordable social security policy and, in particular, providing income support for the elderly, are clear policy priorities for Hong Kong. Developing such policies hinges on the following factors: demographic and economic projections; the degree of income disparity and progressivity of the tax system; the financial position of the government; and the attitude of the business community to social objectives. At present the outlook is for fiscal measures to make only a small contribution to solving Hong Kong's social welfare problems.

Social welfare expenditure has been maintained at a relatively low level, of around 8 per cent of total public expenditure. In fact this share declined for several years after 1988/9, despite claims that more and better social welfare and services to the needy were to be provided. The 1995/6 budget reversed this trend, providing for a rate of increase in expenditure on social welfare greater than for spending as a whole. It is clear, however, that this move did not indicate any long-term intention to substantially increase the commitment of the government to social welfare programmes. Budgets over the next few years are expected to constrain the growth in this area relative to spending on economic development. Moreover, the firm intention to maintain the overall ratio of government spending to GDP at the current low levels imposes an upper limit on the development of social security.

The issues are particularly acute because the Hong Kong population is ageing. Projections based on the 1991 census show that the median age is expected to increase from thirty-two in 1991 to thirty-seven in 2001 and further to forty-one in 2011, while the proportion of those aged sixty-five and over will rise from 9 per cent in 1991 to 12 per cent in 2011, and remain at that level till 2011. As the population ages, demand for welfare services by the elderly will increase sharply.

In the early 1990s, the government recognized the complexities and difficulties of providing adequate income support for an ageing population. An attempt to move forward with a broad-based pension plan met with strong resistence from the business sector and from China. In 1996 the government has settled for mandating membership of private, employer-based pension schemes. This 'solution' has the apparent merit of low cost for the tax system, although a modest 'top up' of schemes may be necessary. It cannot be claimed however that the deeper problem has been solved, since the coverage of the private work-based schemes will not be universal enough to eliminate demands on the social welfare system.

Support for Industrial Restructuring

The Hong Kong government has never pursued an active industrial policy, whether in the early stage of economic development, or in the recent crucial period of economic restructuring. Expenditure on the 'Economic Group' — monetary affairs, food supply, air and sea communications and power, travel and tourism, trade and industry, public safety, and labour — accounts for only 5 per cent of total public expenditure, reflecting this philosophy of minimizing intervention in the business sector.

The manufacturing sector receives only token support for industrial upgrading. Lacking financial support from the government for research and development (R&D), or for adopting advanced technology, the manufacturing sector is gradually losing its technological edge to other newly industrialized economies. The business community has proposed that government should spend the equivalent of 1 per cent of GDP in promoting R&D and industrial training through a matching grant scheme funded equally by the business community and the government. At present, the government spends less than 0.1 per cent of GDP on R&D, and industrial training. The 1 per cent target is a very modest one by international standards. The other three Asian newly industrialized economies have already reached this 1 per cent target and are aiming at a goal of 2 per cent.

Having accumulated huge fiscal reserves, it is unwise for the government not to commit resources to legitimate social needs. Also, its long-held but undue emphasis on financial discipline and neutrality should be reviewed and balanced by consideration of the potential positive effects of well-planned fiscal intervention.

The New Fiscal Constitution

The Basic Law

The PRC will resume the exercise of sovereignty over Hong Kong on 1 July 1997, and will establish the Hong Kong Special Administrative Region (SAR). The SAR will be governed by the Basic Law, a quasi or mini constitution, which specifies the constitutional, political, legal, economic, and social framework governing the operation of the SAR. The following two articles of the chapter on economy of the Basic Law describe the nature of the fiscal policy of the SAR:

> Article 107: The Hong Kong Special Administrative Region shall follow the principle of keeping expenditure within the limits of revenues in drawing up its budget, and strive to achieve a fiscal balance, avoid deficits and keep the budget commensurate with the growth rate of its gross domestic product.

> Article 108: The Hong Kong Special Administrative Region shall practise an independent taxation system. The Hong Kong Special Administrative Region shall, taking the low tax policy previously pursued in Hong Kong as reference, enact laws on its own concerning types of taxes, tax rates, tax reductions, allowances and exemptions, and other matters of taxation.

The aim of Article 107 is to avoid deficits and to achieve fiscal balance. Thus it has been labelled the 'Balanced Budget Article'. The principle specified in Article 107 is similar to the 1986/7 revised budgetary guidelines. However, budgetary guidelines serve as reference for budget formulation, and are subject to regular revision in response to changing social, political, and financial situations. Giving these budgetary guidelines a constitutional status imposes undue restrictions on fiscal policy in Hong Kong, and will affect the formulation and passing of appropriation bills.

The aim of Article 108 is to preserve the present low-tax policy as much as possible after 1997. Any drastic change in tax rates will violate this article. Though the Basic Law is applicable only in the future SAR, the spirit of Article 108 is that the present simple tax system and low tax rate policy should be preserved throughout the final period of British administration. This must exert immense pressure on the formulation of tax policy in the transitional period before and after 1997. During the recent debate on whether the government should set up a taxation review committee, the president of the Taxation Institute of Hong Kong pointed out that any drastic change or overhaul of the existing tax system might not comply with Article 108.

The spirit of Articles 107 and 108 of the Basic Law is not very different from the financial management rules stipulated in the Colonial Regulations. They both aim to establish and preserve the financial viability and stability of the government. The economic stabilization and income redistribution functions of fiscal policy can play only a minimum role in the future SAR government's policy as long as Articles 107 and 108 effectively maintain the *status quo*.

The conservative connotation of these two articles aroused much criticism during the drafting process. The controversy focused on the role of fiscal policy in income redistribution. The business community was very much concerned about the potentially damaging effect on the economy of a more democratic political legislature pressing for higher and progressive tax rates to pay for the expansion of social welfare programmes. These articles were intended to prevent drastic change in Hong Kong's fiscal system, and indirectly, to contain political influences on fiscal policy.

The final version of Articles 107 and 108 represented a compromise by the Basic Law Drafting Committee in which the original more rigid stance was somewhat softened. Even the interpretation of some technical terms of these two articles is a source of dispute. For example, the Chinese authority and the Hong Kong government disagreed over whether the 1992/3 and the 1995/6 budgets followed the 'living within our means' principle. It is probable that Articles 107 and 108 will generate considerable criticism and controversy in the future SAR.

The Memorandum of Understanding

Large-scale, long-term infrastructure projects were proposed in *1989 Governor Wilson's Address*, aiming to lay down a cornerstone for Hong Kong's economic development. One of them was the building of the new airport at Chek Lap Kok. Because the construction and financing of the new airport runs through 1997, the endorsement of the Chinese government is essential to obtain bank loans, attract private investments, and grant franchises. After intensive discussion, the governments of the United Kingdom and the People's Republic of China reached agreement on the new airport and on 3 September 1991 signed the 'Memorandum Of Understanding Concerning The Construction Of The New Airport In Hong Kong And Related Questions' (MOU). The Chinese government promised to support the project. In return, the Hong Kong government made a series of commitments. Those affecting fiscal policy in the transitional period are as follows:

1. The Hong Kong government will be responsible for the construction of the airport project up to 30 June 1997 and will complete the project to the maximum extent possible.
2. The Hong Kong government can borrow money to finance the airport project. As long as the total amount of debt to be repaid after 30 June 1997 does not exceed HK$5 billion, the Hong Kong government is free to borrow as necessary while informing the Chinese government. Borrowing over HK$5 billion will only proceed after obtaining approval from the Chinese government.
3. The Hong Kong government will plan its finance with the firm objective that the fiscal reserves on 30 June 1997 to be left for the use of the Hong Kong Special Administrative Region government will not be less than HK$25 billion.

The above commitments impose significant new constraints on the formulation of fiscal policy, constraints even more restrictive than the internal budgetary guidelines on public debts and fiscal reserves. In order to satisfy the financial obligations of the MOU, financial secretaries will need to control the growth of non-airport related expenditures. Other programmes to support economic development such as the provision of tax incentives and matching grants to encourage research and development, or industrial technical training, that might require a substantial financial commitment from the government, can only hope to get minimal funding. Social welfare spending will also need to be constrained.

The financial obligations of the MOU and the subsequent

negotiation on the financial arrangement indicate that the Chinese government is very concerned about the financial position of the future SAR government. The deadlock of the negotiation between the Chinese government and the Hong Kong government on the new airport hinged on the amount of retained fiscal reserves and the maximum ceiling for outstanding public debt beyond 30 June 1997. The crux of the problem was the budgetary guideline on fiscal reserves. This guideline was for whatever reason not explicitly dealt with when the financial secretary adopted the medium-range forecast in 1986/7. Unfortunately, the Hong Kong government did not accept the Chinese view, arguing that the land fund should be considered together with the fiscal reserves in judging the true financial position of the SAR government after 1997. In one of the scenarios proposed by the Hong Kong government, only HK$5 billion would be left to the SAR government. The financial obligations stipulated in the MOU could be regarded as a compromise between divergent views on the land fund.

The Need for Fiscal Flexibility

The changing demographic, social, and economic environments warrant a more flexible approach in conducting fiscal policy in Hong Kong. This is supported further by the fact that monetary policy in Hong Kong is constrained by the sole objective of maintaining the stability of the external value of the Hong Kong dollar, i.e. the linked exchange rate, leaving other social and economic objectives to be pursued mainly by the fiscal policy. In the past, the primary objective of the tax system and fiscal policy in Hong Kong was to generate sufficient recurrent revenue and fiscal reserves. In an open and gradually democratized society and a mature economy, it is naive to assume that this conservative fiscal policy will remain acceptable. Criticism of the government's handling of retirement protection and industrial upgrading reflects this situation.

A more flexible approach does not necessarily imply a breach of fiscal prudence. Increasing public expenditure will expand the size of the public sector, but this could be financed by increasing tax revenues, keeping the budget in balance. Growth in expenditure might however violate the budgetary criterion that public expenditure growth should not exceed the trend assumption as to growth in GDP. Strictly adhered to, the guideline on total expenditure growth set in 1986/7 means that the public sector share of gross national product (GNP) should only be equal to, or less than, its level at that time i.e. 16.1 per cent. This is a very restrictive constraint, taking no account of changing fiscal needs. Some observers have suggested a ceiling of 20 per cent, while others have proposed an even lower ceiling of 15 per cent. Flexibility requires a higher ceiling. The point is not the definition of an optimal ceiling, but whether the spending is justifiable and affordable.

Many conservatives express concern that deficits will become uncontrollable if active fiscal policy replaces prudent financial management. They argue that the deficit budgets throughout the medium-range forecast period from 1993/4 to 1996/7 indicate how the financial situation of the government is being adversely affected by growing political pressure to increase public expenditure. This argument is unfounded. The projected deficits are mainly to finance capital works for the new airport. Nevertheless, the deficits raise an important issue.

Economic theory argues that long-term, large-scale infrastructure investments should be financed with debt. This spreads the financing cost over time and achieves better intergenerational equity. Unfortunately, this commonly accepted wisdom is not reflected in the MOU, which limits outstanding public bonds beyond 30 June 1997 to HK$5 billion. While this may contain the financial obligation of the future HKSAR government, the limit has a damaging effect on the financial arrangements for the new airport and makes little economic sense. The debt-financed proportion of the deficits forecast over the period of airport construction is much less than the portion financed from non-recurrent expenditure and fiscal reserves. Fortunately, there is still room for manoeuvre through issue of private bonds by the Airport Authority.

The Hong Kong Monetary Authority already issues exchange fund bills and notes as monetary instruments to stabilize the linked exchange rate. The financial secretary should also consider developing the public debt instruments market to enable private pension schemes to hold public, Hong Kong-dollar-denominated bonds as investments and to expand the capital market basis for the conduct of monetary policy. This development would call for a comprehensive review of the philosophy and implementation of fiscal policy in Hong Kong.

There have not been any significant changes to the fiscal system and fiscal policy of Hong Kong since the Second World War. Financial sufficiency and stability have long been the main objectives of the Hong Kong fiscal system. This conservative approach laid down first under the Colonial Regulations, will become counterproductive if the economy and society are to continue to progress.

Angered by the widening income disparity generated by a conservative fiscal policy favouring business, and dissatisfied with the passive role of fiscal policy in promoting social and economic development, political parties and many labour, business, social, and professional organizations are increasingly demanding to be involved in the formulation of fiscal policy. This sentiment was strongly reflected in the number of councillors voting against the 1992/3 budget in the legislature, and in the sensitivity of the government to the new political reality since that episode.

Prior consultation before drafting budgets may ease criticism somewhat. But it is the underlying philosophy of conventional fiscal policy which is at stake. To formulate a budget which can address the short-term and long-term social and economic issues, the role of the Hong Kong government in economic management in the transitional period must be redefined. A more balanced emphasis on efficiency, equity, and the revenue productivity of the fiscal system is preferable to simply focusing on financial stability.

For any reform of fiscal policy to be successful, an understanding and supportive attitude from China is of the utmost importance. The Chinese government has criticized the past several budgets of the Hong Kong government for violating the spirit of Articles 107 and 108 of the Basic Law. Unfortunately, these two conditions are very difficult to satisfy. First, internal consensus on a reformed fiscal policy arrived at through a political process in Hong Kong is virtually impossible to accomplish within the present constitutional set-up. Second, the Chinese authorities insist that the future SAR government be endowed with substantial financial resources.

Eventually, Hong Kong people will press the Hong Kong

government and the future SAR government for policies that require a more flexible fiscal system. How such demands will be received hinges on the response of the evolving political system to the economic challenges in front of us.

4. The Linked Exchange Rate and Macroeconomic Policy

Guobo Huang

F31
E44 E60

This chapter takes up the policy issues centred on, but not restricted to, Hong Kong's linked exchange rate system. These issues include the broad macroeconomic policy choices open to the government, and the narrower question of appropriate monetary arrangements.

The problem of macroeconomic policy always depends on the context. For Hong Kong in the run-up to 1997 and beyond, this context includes increasing political and economic integration with China. Political uncertainties will continue to give rise to economic shocks as the new political relationship with the PRC is worked out. At the same time, economic linkage with China has changed the relationship of the Hong Kong economy with the major Western economies in recent years, making it increasingly dependent on mainland markets. Undoubtedly, this dependence will continue to develop, and will subject Hong Kong to much greater influence from the mainland, both positive and negative. These changes lead to one major question: should Hong Kong's linked exchange rate, which was established to cope with the confidence crisis in the early 1980s, be maintained, be reformed, or be abolished?

Also, problems are emerging that raise questions about the proper macroeconomic role of the government. The most obvious of these problems is persistent inflation, especially high real estate prices and rents. This development has led to calls for the government to opt for greater control of the macroeconomy by reforming the current exchange rate arrangement, an arrangement which now stands in the way of any general monetary management. Any effort to manage the macroeconomy will have to contend with other developments. As the Hong Kong economy becomes more mature, market concentration is increasing in many key industries, including banking and real estate, replacing competitive market pricing with less flexible price-making by oligopolies. The flexibility of labour markets is also likely to be impaired as a high value-added service economy replaces an economy based on labour-intensive manufacturing.

Any study of Hong Kong's macroeconomic policy problems must begin from a basic understanding of the historical arrangements of the Hong Kong dollar, and the policy options under the current exchange rate. Then, in light of the political and economic changes now taking place, we can consider: the trade-offs between maintaining the linked exchange rate and scrapping it; alternatives for reforming the current system; the possible role of fiscal policy; and the role of Hong Kong Monetary Authority (HKMA).

The Hong Kong Dollar's Historical Arrangements

From 1935 to 1972, Hong Kong maintained an exchange rate arrangement called the 'Pound Sterling Standard', following the currency board approach. Under this arrangement, the Hong Kong dollar maintained a fixed exchange rate to the pound sterling and 100 per cent sterling reserves were required for outstanding Hong Kong dollars.

Along with other 'Pound Zone' currencies, the Hong Kong dollar was delinked from sterling in 1972, when sterling was floated against the US dollar. The Hong Kong dollar was pegged immediately to the US dollar, at a rate of HK$5.65 per US dollar. This arrangement did not last long. As the Bretton Woods system broke down, the US dollar depreciated sharply against most other major currencies. The Hong Kong dollar was first appreciated against the US dollar, then finally in 1973, it was permitted to float.

The Hong Kong dollar then enjoyed ten years of freedom from control. Until 1983 the exchange rates against other currencies were determined by demand and supply. The Exchange Fund intervened in the market only under special circumstances. No foreign exchange reserves were required from the issuing banks against Hong Kong dollar-note issues and the Hong Kong dollar was no longer backed by foreign currencies. However, the Exchange Fund still existed, and continued to hold foreign exchange reserves.

Since October 1983, the Hong Kong dollar has been linked once more to the US dollar, this time at a rate of HK$7.8 per US dollar. In 1973 when the Hong Kong dollar was floated, it was the violent fluctuations of the US dollar that made it an unsuitable key-currency link. In 1983, it was speculation and loss of confidence in the Hong Kong dollar that forced it to be pegged again to the US dollar. The direct cause of this weakness was the deadlocked Sino-British negotiations over Hong Kong's future. From July to September 1983, the Hong Kong dollar depreciated by 38.4 per cent against the US dollar, compared with the depreciation of 22 per cent from March 1977 to June 1982.

The new linked exchange rate works in a way very similar to the previous linkage to sterling. For every HK$7.8 issued by the banks, US$1 must be deposited with the Exchange Fund. Hong Kong dollar currency is thus 100 per cent guaranteed by foreign exchange reserves. Similarly, for every HK$7.8 recovered by the issuing banks and put out of circulation, US$1 is claimed back from the Fund.

The fixed exchange rate available to the note-issuing banks ensures that the market exchange rate between the Hong Kong dollar and the US dollar will not deviate from the linked rate in the long run. However, in the short run, there can still be small differences between the two rates, differences that arbitrage does not eliminate. Reasons for deviations include the fact that any arbitrage must be conducted using cash and that only the issuing banks can deal with the Fund at the link rate.

To control the short-term deviations of the telegraphic transfer market rate from the link rate in the foreign exchange market and related fluctuations in interbank interest rates, several changes to Hong Kong's monetary arrangements have been made in recent years. These developments include: (1) the new 'accounting arrangements' established in July 1988 between the management bank of the Clearing House of the Hong Kong Association of Banks (HongkongBank) and the Exchange Fund, giving the Exchange Fund leverage over the liquidity of the banking system; (2) the sale of Exchange Fund Bills beginning in March 1990, establishing a powerful open-market operation instrument; and (3) the introduction of a liquidity adjustment facility in June 1992, adding a discount window facility to the instruments available to the newly established HKMA.

Monetary Policy with a Linked Exchange Rate

The linkage arrangement maintains a fixed exchange rate between the Hong Kong dollar and the US dollar. The Hong Kong dollar floats with the US dollar against other major currencies. Because the Hong Kong economy is very small compared to that of the United States, it does not affect the US economy significantly; economic events in the United States, however, have important effects on Hong Kong.

One important consequence of the US dollar link, a consequence that is a vital element in analysing the Hong Kong economy, is that Hong Kong's interest rates cannot deviate by a big margin from US interest rates. It is easy to understand why. There is nearly 'perfect capital mobility' between Hong Kong and the United States; that is, investors in capital and money markets can shift funds between the two regions without regulatory restrictions. In this environment, the most important factor determining international investment is the expected return on Hong Kong's assets relative to the expected return on foreign assets. Because the exchange rate is fixed, there is no exchange rate risk. Any difference in the interest rates of the two regions will induce sales of the low-return asset and purchases of the high-return asset until any difference is eliminated. Where the asset is very easily and cheaply traded — wholesale bank deposits, for example — these shifts in funds occur so smoothly that interest rates must always be virtually identical.

Monetary Policy Operations

The effective linkage of Hong Kong interest rates to those in the United States places a severe constraint on Hong Kong's policy makers. Monetary policies that aim to control the macroeconomy require a monetary authority (not necessarily a central bank), a set of monetary instruments (open market operations, discount window, reserve requirement, central bank lending, etc.), certain targets (interest rates, prices, economic growth, internal and external balance etc.), and mechanisms that transmit policy moves to the economy.

A discussion of monetary policy in Hong Kong might seem irrelevant, since Hong Kong does not have a central bank. This is a misunderstanding. For one thing, the HKMA plays some of the roles of a central bank. These roles could be easily extended into the area of aggregate monetary control, if appropriate. In any case, it does no harm to consider what a potential central bank could do in Hong Kong, and how this relates to existing monetary arrangements.

Disappointingly, the conclusion is that under conditions of Hong Kong's perfect capital mobility and the linked exchange rate system, monetary policy could not be effective. Assume that the authorities, facing a high inflation rate, attempt to tighten liquidity by selling Foreign Exchange Fund bills to absorb public holdings of cash. This should lead to a reduction in the availability of credit and in currency in circulation, and a higher interest rate. Tight money and high interest rates might then help to moderate inflation as consumption and investment expenditures fell easing demand pressure.

However, before any of these effects could take place, higher Hong Kong dollar interest rates will lead investors to shift funds into Hong Kong dollar assets. Foreign exchange will be sold for Hong Kong dollars. The supply of Hong Kong dollars will increase and will stop increasing only when Hong Kong's interest rate is the same as the US interest rate. But once this is the case, the money supply will have reverted to its old level, and the authorities' initiative to control money supply will have been in vain.

In summary, the only change will be an increase in the foreign exchange held in Hong Kong. Because the authorities have to maintain the link, they cannot change the money supply or the interest rate. As a consequence, demand and income pressure producing inflation cannot be reduced through monetary policy.

Should the Linked Exchange Rate be Abolished?

People arguing that the linkage arrangement should be abandoned completely point to the policy freedom otherwise available. Under a floating exchange rate system, the authorities can manage the money supply and the interest rate. As a result, monetary policy becomes very powerful. Look again at the policy problem considered above — high inflation.

If the authorities start to cut the money supply to cool down the economy, Hong Kong interest rates will rise, and funds will begin to shift into Hong Kong dollar-denominated assets. In contrast to the earlier case, this shift will push the Hong Kong dollar to appreciate in the foreign exchange market. Without the commitment to a fixed exchange rate, the authorities do not have to buy up the extra foreign exchange and do not have to release domestic currency into the market. The interest rate increase will not be reversed. Meanwhile, the appreciation of the currency will supply an additional check on demand for Hong Kong goods and services by encouraging imports and discouraging exports. A flexible exchange rate, therefore, might give Hong Kong a potentially powerful monetary authority armed with effective monetary instruments.

There is an additional advantage to exchange rate flexibility. A flexible exchange rate can prevent the transmission of foreign inflationary (or deflationary) pressure to the Hong Kong economy. When the United States reduces its interest rate to stimulate its economy, funds will flow to Hong Kong. Under a fixed exchange rate, this inflow will depress Hong Kong interest rates and accelerate inflation in Hong Kong. With a floating exchange rate, Hong Kong interest rates can be managed by the monetary authority and the Hong Kong dollar allowed to appreciate, easing the inflationary pressure by reducing the demand for Hong Kong produced goods.

The final outcome, as the Hong Kong economy responds to the external shock, in this case a fall in US interest rates, depends on the policy pursued by the monetary authority. If they have adopted some target for the level of the money stock, the reduction in Hong Kong's income will eventually exert downward pressure on money demand and the interest rate. At the end of the process, Hong Kong will have a lower interest rate, lower income, and an appreciated exchange rate. But there will be no increase in inflation. If the monetary authority targets interest rates, at the end of the process there will be an appreciated exchange rate, lower income, and a lower money stock. Whatever the exact choices, exchange rate flexibility allows the authority to conduct independent monetary policies.

Protection Offered by the Linkage Arrangement

The above argument offers a strong case for ending the exchange rate link. But there are other important considerations to take into account, especially as we approach 1997.

The most important role of the link is the psychological stability that results from the guaranteed convertibility of Hong Kong dollars. With the link and the 100 per cent foreign exchange back-up, the Hong Kong dollar is not vulnerable to speculation in the foreign exchange market. In a crisis, people are sure that they can convert their Hong Kong currency into foreign exchange at the fixed rate. A crisis is less likely to lead to a run on the banks, or exert sudden pressure on the foreign exchange market. Hong Kong immigrants and businesses remain confident that they can convert their Hong Kong dollars into any currency they want. Even in the event of sudden panic buying of foreign exchange, the Exchange Fund would still be able to satisfy the demand at the fixed rate.

Even though Hong Kong currency is backed fully by reserves of foreign exchange, there might be concern over the huge volume of Hong Kong dollar deposits, that are not backed in the same way. If all Hong Kong dollar deposits were withdrawn to buy foreign exchange, there would not be sufficient reserves to meet all demands at the linked rate. A threat to convertibility might arise either from the action of the depository institutions (chiefly the banks), or from the actions of individual depositors.

So far as depository institutions are concerned, their ability to mount a run on the Hong Kong dollar is limited. Firstly, at any time, most deposits will have been lent out, leaving depository institutions with only limited liquidity in the form of a clearing position. Moreover, they must maintain an adequate level of Hong Kong dollar cash to meet local demands. This level of liquidity will rise in periods of volatility. If the banks borrow Hong Kong dollar deposits for conversion to foreign exchange, the interbank borrowing rate (HIBOR) will be pushed higher. It is also open to the HKMA to further drain liquidity out of the banking system forcing up the HIBOR to levels high enough to control speculation.

Since the banks are aware of the possible action of the authorities and the potentially high borrowing costs, they must think twice before under-taking speculative moves.

From the point of view of depositors, it must be recognized that if they suddenly withdraw all deposits or even a significant share of deposits, the problem is not one of an exchange rate crisis, but one of a banking crisis. The problem for banks is that their assets, typically deposits, are short term, but their liabilities, typically loans, are long term and cannot be recovered at short notice. A crisis of confidence in the currency might cause a run on all banks. If deposits are withdrawn sufficiently gradually, banks can recover loans and pay out cash withdrawals to depositors. Over time, a multiple contraction process for bank credit (both deposits and loans) occurs. At the limit, such a contraction leaves only the initial currency, currency fully backed by foreign exchange. Thus full backing of currency amounts to full backing of all Hong Kong dollar money. Also, with the link and the full backing of the Hong Kong dollar currency, there is much less chance of a general loss of confidence and panic run on the banks.

It must be stressed that the full convertibility of the Hong Kong dollar at a fixed rate guarantees only the immediate interests of currency holders. It does not mean that the economy might not suffer disastrous consequences from the wholesale conversion of Hong Kong dollars into foreign currencies. As Hong Kong dollars are exchanged for other currencies, local money supply and total purchasing power will fall. Demand for goods, services, and assets, especially real estate, would drop, with the possibility of rapid deflation. Convertibility of the Hong Kong dollar at a fixed rate can only guarantee the value of the cash held. But since few people nowadays hold the bulk of their wealth in cash, convertibility alone cannot protect them from losses caused by deflation. Despite this limitation, the linkage is still valuable to the extent that it stands in the way of sudden panic, and minimizes losses if funds did flow out of the economy in a crisis.

The advantages of convertibility have been recognized by many other small economies that peg their exchange rates to one key currency, or to a basket of foreign currencies. This is not because these economies do not want to have more power to pursue independent monetary policies. However, for small economies, the costs of exchange rate volatility, and the costs involved in stabilizing the exchange rate often outweigh the gains from a flexible rate. Markets for goods and financial assets in small countries lack 'depth' and 'breadth', leaving them especially vulnerable to shocks from a volatile exchange rate. Such volatility can be caused by both internal and external events, and by pure speculation in the market. Stability in the external sector is vital, in these circumstances.

For Hong Kong, this argument holds with special force. Hong Kong's high degree of openness and extremely shallow internal market means that the economy is very vulnerable to external volatility. A flexible exchange rate would greatly increase this volatility. Another familiar factor is that Hong Kong will be returned to China in 1997, and is in a very sensitive transition period. Given the political uncertainties, uncertainties that will not end in 1997, the current exchange rate arrangement will undoubtedly greatly enhance confidence in the currency, and confidence in foreign and local investment in Hong Kong.

Also, Hong Kong's extreme economic openness, small internal market, and near perfect capital mobility reduce the value of an independent monetary policy. Even with a floating exchange rate, the Hong Kong economy cannot be insulated from external pressures. Monetary policy has only limited room to manoeuvre (especially in the long run), and it may be better to rely on the flexibility of private markets in adjusting to shocks than on the wisdom of policy makers. Even on purely economic grounds, a linked rate may still be preferable.

Although, all in all, the advantages of the link obviously outweigh the disadvantages and the linkage system should be maintained, some may argue that there could be useful reforms within the link framework. These include adjusting the full foreign exchange back-up of Hong Kong currency, introducing some flexibility into the setting of the peg rate, and adjusting the currency to which the Hong Kong dollar is pegged.

An End to 100 Per Cent Foreign Exchange Back-Up

The world economy said goodbye to the gold or silver standard system many years ago. It is almost out of the question for any country to return to a 100 per cent gold or silver reserve for its paper currency. Most currencies adopting a fixed exchange rate do not have 100 per cent back-up and may not have any gold and silver reserve backing at all. Reserves are held to support confidence in the currency relative to other currencies, and as a check on the government's behaviour, particularly its spending. If the authorities have enough foreign exchange reserves to intervene in the market and to stabilize the fixed rate within a narrow range, this level of reserves is sufficient. Theory, and empirical studies from other countries, suggest that reserve holdings are positively related to an economy's level of imports, its propensity to import, the volatility of the balance of payments, the opportunity cost of holding reserves, and so on.

While 100 per cent back-up gives 100 per cent confidence, which is welcome, such a system has high costs. Huge sums that could be used in economic development and welfare are tied up simply to prevent a run on the currency. Although foreign exchange reserves can be invested in financial markets to earn a yield, such investment has to be on a very liquid basis to provide immediate access, or access at short notice, to foreign currency. This feature restricts the rate of return on reserves. Relative to the size of the Hong Kong economy, the foreign exchange held with the Foreign Exchange Fund is a very large amount. The cost of these holdings in lost investment opportunities is therefore also considerable. Who pays this cost?

Bank notes are essentially loans from holders of the notes to the issuing banks. Thus the stable part of currency in circulation represents a permanent interest-free loan by the public to the issuing banks. But the issuing banks in Hong Kong do not derive any direct benefit from this. Under the current arrangements, the currency-issuing banks are not paid interest on their deposits of foreign exchange with the Exchange Fund in return for the Certificate of Indebtedness that permit them to issue Hong Kong dollar currency. The issuing banks neither gain nor lose, except to the extent that they incur costs in handling the currency and obtain compensatory benefits by publishing their names on bank notes and enjoying a special status as an issuing bank. The Exchange Fund earns any income on the investment of the foreign exchange (though the performance is poor, restricted by liquidity requirements).

This arrangement could be changed to allow the issuing banks to earn interest on the foreign exchange they deposit, redistributing the cost between the issuing banks and the Exchange Fund. But taking the Hong Kong economy as a whole, the opportunity cost of holding 100 per cent foreign exchange back-up for local currency cannot be escaped. In effect, it is the foreign central banks that issue the foreign exchange held by the Exchange Fund that enjoy the benefit of the interest-free loan represented by the currency. If we assume that most of the foreign exchange held by the Fund is in US dollars, then holders of Hong Kong dollars are making interest-free loans to the US government.

The Hong Kong dollar is now circulating widely in Guangdong province and other adjacent regions. The trend is for an increase in this Hong Kong dollar outflow. There have even been suggestions that the Hong Kong dollar become the legal tender for the region. As the regional use of Hong Kong currency increases, an increasing amount of foreign exchange will be required to back it. This constitutes additional pressure on the foreign exchange resources of the issuing banks and on Hong Kong as a whole. It might be the right time to ask whether the 100 per cent back-up is becoming too costly as a means to support the stability of the currency in Hong Kong.

An Adjustable Peg Rate

As is well known, the Hong Kong dollar/US dollar exchange rate has been fixed at 7.8 since the linked exchange rate system was established in 1983. Should this rate be subject to reviews and adjustments from time to time?

Fixed exchange rates may need realignment to reflect changes in the fundamental factors determining the appropriate rate. Otherwise, even if the authorities succeed in intervening in the market and pegging the rate at a certain level in the short run, speculation will build up in the long run and may eventually defeat efforts to fix a rate at the target level. The collapse of the Bretton Woods system and the break-up of the exchange rate mechanism of the EEC provide good examples of the possible difficulties.

Factors determining the long-run exchange rate include the purchasing power of a currency, productivity, and international competitiveness. When a country's inflation is consistently higher than other countries, its currency should tend to depreciate. Higher productivity means lower prices and greater competitiveness. This should tend to appreciate the currency. If two similarly important countries fix their mutual exchange rate, to avoid realignment, their economies, especially their inflation rates, must move together. Where a smaller country's currency is pegged to a major economy's currency, as in the case of Hong Kong, its inflation rate should be similar to that of the major economy.

Hong Kong's annual inflation rate has been, on average, 5 per cent higher than the US inflation rate over the past decade. This suggests that its currency should have depreciated against the US dollar to the same extent. However, despite the higher inflation rate in Hong Kong, the exchange rate remains unchanged. This has led to doubt whether the current rate of 7.8 is now realistic, and to proposals that the linkage rate should be adjusted from time to time to reflect the disparity.

How can we explain the disparity in the inflation rates of Hong Kong and the United States under the fixed linkage rate? One important point to note is that the high inflation rate is consistent with the linkage in the sense that money supply growth is subject to zero control from the government. Inflation requires adequate monetary growth to sustain it. Under the linked exchange rate, if that growth is insufficient, the resulting lack of liquidity and tendency for interest rates to rise results in an inflow into Hong Kong dollar assets. As the HKMA resists any appreciation that develops, the supply of Hong Kong dollars increases and inflation continues without constraint.

But how can the Hong Kong inflation rate be higher than the US inflation rate in the first place? With the exchange rate fixed, higher inflation in Hong Kong will make goods in Hong Kong more expensive. 'Goods-market arbitrage' — cheaper imports, and less competitive exports, should bring local prices back to a level comparable with world prices. If the linkage rate was set at the correct level at the outset, then either the subsequent excess inflation rate should not have developed, or the link rate should not have been sustainable.

However, many goods and services consumed in Hong Kong cannot be imported. These are the so-called 'non-tradeables', goods and services produced and consumed locally such as real estate and restaurant meals. Even where the import price of tradeable goods remains comparable to international prices, the sales price in Hong Kong reflects big mark-ups, justified by high rents and operational costs including wages. But there is still an unexplained problem. The high price of non-tradables should greatly impair the international competitiveness of goods from Hong Kong, because labour and other costs have inflated. A strong demand for imported goods and weak exports should lead to unbalanced trade and deficits, should undermine the confidence of foreign capital, and should finally put pressure on the exchange rate to depreciate.

This did not happen for two main reasons. One is that Hong Kong has shifted much of its production to factories in China. These factories employ millions of low-wage workers and take advantage of low taxes, low rent, and low operation costs. This production is insulated from rising costs in Hong Kong and remains very competitive in international markets. Meanwhile, the repatriation of profits from the mainland has greatly supported the Hong Kong economy.

The other factor is that as an international financial centre, Hong Kong has been attracting huge capital inflows. The rapid run-up in the prices of non-tradeables, especially real estate, has not so far deterred this inflow. In fact asset price increases have provided good investment opportunities. As a result, international capital has often exerted pressure on the Hong Kong dollar to appreciate rather than depreciate. Also, at least so far, Hong Kong's status as a re-export centre, and as a shopping and tourist location, has been largely immune from the impact of rising local prices, giving additional support to the economy.

Given that the impact of rising prices on Hong Kong's competitiveness has not reduced demand growth and slowed inflation, should Hong Kong reserve the option of adjusting the pegged rate if necessary? This author does not recommend this. For one thing, any change in the par must affect people's confidence in the pegged rate and lead to an expectation of further adjustments. Such uncertainty might also give rise to speculation and finally to the collapse of the system.

When a fundamental disequilibrium occurs, realignment of the nominal exchange rate is not the only solution. The other possibility is to correct any disequilibrium by fundamental economic adjustments. Maintaining the fixed nominal exchange rate must, in time, force the real economy to adjust to the linked rate. A better policy approach is for the government to do what it can to suppress the inflation of the non-tradeables prices. Possible measures include increasing the supply of land, reducing wage inflation and inflation of government-controlled industries, controlling speculation on real estate, and adopting a more suitable fiscal policy.

Alternatives to the US Dollar as the Link Currency

The Hong Kong dollar has been pegged to the US dollar since the link was set up. The usual consideration for choosing a suitable currency peg is that the currency be a major international currency with a stable value and strong support from its national economy. In particular, this economy should be the major trading partner of the local economy to obtain the maximum benefit from the stable exchange rate between the two economies. The Hong Kong dollar was pegged to the US dollar for exactly these economic reasons.

Another option is to peg the home currency to a basket of major foreign currencies. The currencies in the basket should still be chosen following the above criteria. Normally, the weight of the various currencies in the basket depends on their importance in the trade of the home country. The advantage of this arrangement is that although the home country is still affected directly by the countries in the basket, the exchange rate fluctuations related to factors specific to one economy are reduced.

While adopting a basket of currencies to which the Hong Kong dollar would be pegged is a relevant alternative, it is not without disadvantages. On the positive side, it would reduce the influence of US economic fluctuations on Hong Kong. As we mentioned above, in recent years, the Hong Kong economy has become more integrated with mainland China's economy, and no longer follows the US economic cycle to the same extent as in the past. US policies have an increasingly negative effect on Hong Kong. Also, bringing the renminbi into the currency basket will allow for the growing impact of the Chinese economy on local economic conditions.

On the negative side, pegging the Hong Kong dollar to a basket of currencies is difficult to operate in practice, demanding constant management and administration. It is much less direct, transparent, and automatic than the current system. A simple, transparent system is always preferable. At the same time, while including the renminbi in the currency basket might be appropriate in the very long run, there are problems in implementing this in the near future. In particular, the renminbi and the Chinese economy are not yet sufficiently stable. Also it will take time before the renminbi is fully convertible and it will take even longer for the renminbi to be recognized internationally as a major currency able to support confidence in the Hong Kong dollar. In addition, combining renminbi with the US dollar may not make much practical difference because the United States has been, and will continue to be, the major trading partner of China, so that the renminbi has been, and will continue to be, managed mainly in relation to the US dollar. Changes in renminbi against other currencies largely follow changes in the US dollar against other currencies.

Finally, the main problem created by the link with the US dollar has been the impact of US monetary policy. But US economic conditions are more or less in line with those of other major economies. Even if the Hong Kong dollar is linked to a basket of currencies, much of the impact on Hong Kong of international economic shocks cannot be escaped. Taking into account all these factors, linking the Hong Kong dollar to a basket of currencies may be useful in the longer run, when Hong Kong has worked through the present transition period, when the Hong Kong economy has become further integrated with China, and when the renminbi has become more stable and enjoys convertibility. In the short run, it cannot be recommended.

In summary, it appears that the current fixed-rate link with the US dollar backed-up by 100 per cent foreign exchange reserves is for now the best option. As long as this is the case, an independent monetary policy for Hong Kong will not be possible. This does not mean however that there are no areas where government macroeconomic policy needs review, nor does it mean that the role of the HKMA needs no extension.

Fiscal Policy with a Fixed Exchange Rate

It was argued above that under the linked exchange rate, the HKMA has no control over money supply or the interest rate. But this does not mean that abolishing the linked exchange rate is the only way to bring the Hong Kong economy, especially the inflation rate, under control. One possibility often ignored is the use of fiscal policy — the management of demand through adjustment in taxation and expenditures. In principal, fiscal policy has a very powerful influence on aggregate demand and inflation under a fixed exchange rate, particularly when demand and inflation are high.

Where the exchange rate floats, any effort to control inflation by adjusting government net spending downward may run into problems because the moderation in spending tends to reduce interest rates (hence encouraging private consumption and investment). With a fixed exchange rate, as was explained above, any tendency for interest rates to adjust is counteracted in international capital markets. As government spending contracts, the contraction is accommodated by the monetary contraction necessary to keep interest rates stable. On the other hand, when the government increases its expenditures, as the Hong Kong government is now doing on the new airport, the related demand growth is not dampened by any tendency for interest rates to increase. Any tendency for interest rates to rise attracts funds to Hong Kong dollar assets, increasing the money supply and restoring interest rate parity.

Thus, although near-perfect capital mobility and a linked exchange rate means that monetary policy is not effective, fiscal policy can be a powerful instrument for macroeconomic control. Moreover with the link in place, the budgetary position of the government, whether directed at macroeconomic objectives or not, is likely to have a strong impact on the economy.

Fiscal Policy as an Offset to the Effects of the Link

The difficulties created by the linked exchange rate itself strengthen the argument for increased attention to fiscal policy in Hong Kong. Besides eliminating the option of an independent monetary policy, maintaining the link commits Hong Kong to the consequences of US monetary policy choices.

Firstly, the fact that Hong Kong's interest rate cannot deviate from the US interest rate has profound effects. The interest rate has a critically important influence on consumption and investment behaviour in a monetary economy. When the US economy was in recession in the early 1990s, interest rates were reduced to a low level to encourage demand. But Hong Kong's economy was not in recession. On the contrary, it put up a strong performance, supported by the fast-growing economy of China. Given low nominal interest rates and the higher Hong Kong inflation rate, the real (inflation adjusted) interest rate has been negative. This has stimulated consumption and investment and worsened inflation. Low interest rates lead to heavy borrowing. Using mortgage loans to speculate in the real estate market is typically stimulated by the low real interest rate. High inflation further reduces the real interest rate, encourages additional demand, and results in even higher inflation. A vicious circle comes into play.

On the other hand, if inflationary pressure in the US now increases, the Federal Reserve may tighten monetary control and increase interest rates. In this event, Hong Kong will also have to raise interest rates. Suppose the economy of mainland China enters a recession. Hong Kong's economy will suffer and will be unable to adopt the low interest rates it requires to support demand. Because the Hong Kong and US economies are often in different stages of the business cycle and are driven by different forces, the concurrent level and movements in their interest rates may well have an undesirable effect.

Secondly, since the Hong Kong dollar is pegged to the US dollar, it floats together with the US dollar against other currencies. When the US dollar is affected by US domestic factors, such as bad economic prospects or low interest rates, the Hong Kong dollar will also depreciate against other currencies. For example, as the trade war between the US and Japan depreciated, the US dollar against the Japanese yen in mid-1994, the Hong Kong dollar also depreciated against the yen. The link disconnects the value of the Hong Kong dollar from Hong Kong's own economic and financial situation. The Hong Kong dollar can exhibit unwanted and unjustified fluctuations against other major currencies. A depreciating US dollar (thus Hong Kong dollar) directly raises Hong Kong's import prices from countries other than the United States, and an appreciating US dollar discourages Hong Kong's exports to these countries.

Despite these arguments indicating that fiscal policy could be effective and useful, and despite the fact that fiscal policy instruments are readily available, fiscal policy has not been actively used by the Hong Kong government, nor has it paid serious attention to the inflationary consequences of recent taxation and expenditure decisions. Ironically, on some occasions this has been regarded as part of its 'non-intervention policy'. Under the 'non-intervention' policy, the budget's only aim has been to make ends meet. We do not debate here whether this was historically right or wrong. The important point is that the government's income and expenditure has effects on the economy far too important to ignore.

It is unduly dogmatic to overemphasize the role of the monetary side in dealing with problems like inflation and rising property prices. Hong Kong is basically a full-employment economy, as its low unemployment rate indicates. Land and housing supply is running far behind strong and rapidly increasing demand. Nevertheless, the Hong Kong government is spending heavily. Among the many investment projects is the US$100 billion new airport. Such heavy spending in a full-employment economy must drive up prices. These price increases cannot be constrained by monetary policy given the exchange rate linkage. Considerations must be paid to macro and structural demand considerations. For example, while spending heavily on the new airport (which it deems necessary), the government could cut its spending on other projects, or could introduce a programme to privatize government-provided housing to absorb private purchasing power.

The Role of the Hong Kong Monetary Authority

The role and status of the HKMA, although controversial, are simple under the current system. As we pointed out above, with the link in place, the HKMA has no power to pursue macroeconomic targets through monetary adjustments, even if it wanted to. Moreover, in the longer run, we do not need the HKMA to 'defend' the linked exchange rate system. The 100 per cent foreign exchange back-up of Hong Kong dollar notes guarantees that the system can defend itself. As a consequence, at the aggregate level and in the longer run, there is no role for the HKMA to play in macroeconomic control. If the HKMA is to have a role at the aggregate level, the replacement of the linked exchange rate by a flexible rate is a prerequisite.

Although the HKMA does not have a role to play in controlling aggregate demand in the longer run, it still has important duties in the short run, and in areas other than aggregate demand management.

The first responsibility is to maintain short-run stability in financial markets. The HKMA needs to play an active role here because the interbank market may be affected by short-term shocks, causing liquidity problems for the banks, pushing the interbank interest rate (HIBOR) to extremely high or low levels. For example, new public offerings of shares often lead to oversubscription. For two or three days, the liquidity of banks may be squeezed, as clients' funds are concentrated in the hands of the agent banks. Before this liquidity can be released to the interbank market, the HKMA may need to intervene to restore liquidity to the system and bring down the HIBOR from a harmful level.

The HKMA's temporary intervention may also be called for because the arbitrage mechanism maintaining the linked exchange rate does not work perfectly in the very short term. Arbitrage between the free foreign exchange market and the Exchange Fund can be undertaken only with cash, and through the currency-issuing banks. Not all the banks have the large cash holdings necessary for effective arbitrage. Even if they have it, they cannot deal with the Exchange Fund directly at the guaranteed 7.8 rate. Only the issuing banks can do this. Besides, when funds flow into and out of Hong Kong dollar assets, they are converted by paying or accepting Hong Kong dollar deposits. The indirect relationship between cash and deposits further complicates and delays the arbitrage process. All these factors mean that the market rate in the short term can deviate from the linked rate. When there are large shifts in funds, the deviation can be substantial. This calls for direct intervention in the interbank market or the foreign exchange market by the HKMA and its Exchange Fund.

A second potential area of responsibility for the HKMA is to conduct some of the normal functions of a central bank: the management of a clearing system, banking for the government, and bank supervision. An efficient interbank clearing system is essential for an efficient banking system. Besides, the way the clearing system is operated affects the operations of the monetary authorities. In Hong Kong, HongkongBank operates the clearing system. All clearing banks must hold their clearing positions with HongkongBank, which, in turn, deposits an equivalent amount with the Exchange Fund. The HKMA can affect the liquidity position of the banks by deciding whether to reinject this fund into the banking system or not. Under this system, HongkongBank is in an advantageous position. It decides the adequacy of other banks' clearing positions, and it has privileged knowledge of the clearing positions and flow of funds of other banks. To end the special historical role of HongkongBank in the banking system, the HKMA should replace the bank as an operator of the clearing system. This would provide the HKMA with a direct way to intervene in the interbank market, assisting it to stabilize interest rates and the exchange rate.

Guaranteeing a fair, efficient, sound, and stable banking system is the objective of any bank regulator. Hong Kong has developed a rather extensive regulatory framework in the last few decades, including entry constraints, price controls, product line control, ratio constraints, and other quantitative and qualitative controls. However, some unjustifiable and unfair practices have been sometimes interpreted as necessary to maintain financial stability and the linked exchange rate. In particular, the interest rate agreement established by the Hong Kong Association of Banks (HKAB), requiring all licensed banks in Hong Kong to pay no interest on current accounts and a fixed rate on savings accounts, has been represented as indispensable in defending the linked rate. This is at best a misunderstanding.

The agreement was established in 1964, long before the current linked rate was introduced. In fact, without the artificial control of interest rates by the agreement, interest rate parity between the United States and Hong Kong would still be automatically established by arbitrage. So long as the Hong

Kong dollar is 100 per cent backed by foreign currency, it is impossible for the Hong Kong interest rate to increase to a level that threatens the linked rate. Fixing interest rates only artificially causes non-price competition among the banks and leads to losses for consumers. Luckily, the government is now set to abolish interest rate control in stages.

Another issue is information disclosure. Information available to the public about banks is much more limited in Hong Kong than in many other developed countries. Such information includes the level of banks' inner reserves, the breakdown of revenue and expenses, loan-loss reserves and non-performing loans, debt maturities, loan portfolios, etc. The argument for maintaining secrecy is that more disclosure will destroy the public's confidence, causing bank runs and instability in the banking system. Again, this is a misunderstanding. Distrust of the public's judgement and denial of the market's capacity to 'supervise' poor management of banks are the basis of this argument, and are dangerously wrong. Serious problems are associated with such 'asymmetric information', including adverse selection and moral hazard.

Concluding Remarks

The linked exchange rate system has provided an anchor stabilizing Hong Kong's economic and financial conditions. Although it has also produced undesirable consequences, the benefits of abandoning or reforming the link must not be exaggerated, and must be balanced against the advantages of keeping the system intact.

It should be noted that given Hong Kong's small economy and its high degree of dependence on other countries, even if the linked exchange rate were abandoned, the room for monetary policy to play a useful role would remain very restricted, while the cost — the exchange rate volatility likely with a floating rate — might be very great. Even when Hong Kong has completed its political transition, a freely floating currency will not be a good choice. A better option is to try to make improvements in other ways.

The HKMA's role in stabilizing the short-term markets, and its development of central bank functions other than long-run macroeconomic management should be further pursued.

Aggregate and structural fiscal policies must be stressed and could play a much bigger role in combating high demand, inflation, and increasing real estate prices.

Before 1997 there is a special need to maintain the link as it exists. Any change would be very sensitive and might lead to destabilizing expectations of more radical moves. After 1997, depending on economic and political circumstances, reform of the system, such as diluting the 100 per cent foreign exchange back-up and linking the Hong Kong dollar to a basket of currencies can be considered.

5. Labour Market Policies in a Changing Political Economy

Ho Lok Sang

Government intervention in the Hong Kong labour market is already fairly extensive. The long-service payment, in force since 1986 and amended several times in favour of the labour force, provides for the payment of two-thirds of the last month's wage times the number of years of service, for workers 'in long service with the same employer', under certain conditions. The Employment Ordinance provides for statutory holidays, annual leave, rest days, maternity leave, and sick leave. The Factory Inspectorate of the Labour Department enforces the Factories and Industrial Undertakings Ordinance and other regulations for industrial safety. The Occupational Health Division of the Labour Department oversees standards and practices for occupational health. Employees' compensation is yet another area in which the Labour Department takes a predominant role. Since 1989 the government has by stages introduced a labour importation scheme. Since 1993 the government has set up an Employees Retraining Board to provide retraining for workers displaced in declining industries and, more recently, for disadvantaged workers.

In recent years, the government has improved on its provisions for severance pay and the long service payment, mandated more holidays for workers, and mandated industrial safety rules, in addition to introducing other pro-labour policies.

These policies reflect, in part, a natural desire to share the benefits of Hong Kong's increasing wealth among more people and, in part, a shift in the political environment with the emergence of more powerful pro-labour pressure groups and of political parties seeking broad community support. But it is important to recognize that however well intentioned, government intervention is costly, and is not justified unless the cost of the identified market failure is greater than the cost of the intervention.

How shall we evaluate the large variety of current and proposed labour-market policies? The next section presents a general framework for analysing labour-market policies. Some guiding principles emerge from the discussion. The chapter then takes up six specific, topical problems as illustrative cases for discussion: labour importation; training; wage subsidies for disadvantaged workers; unemployment protection; minimum wage legislation; and labour relations.

A General Framework

Two strands of economic theory are particularly useful for analysing labour market policies; these are, respectively, the theory of 'externalities' and the 'capital theory' of labour. Externalities are simply the impacts, positive and negative, of private, market-driven decisions on other members of the community. The capital theory of labour stresses the similarity between investment in worker skills and any other investment decision. Unifying these theories is the familiar tool of cost-benefit analysis.

In general, private-sector decision-makers only take account of their private costs and benefits, but private decisions may well have external benefits and costs. A decision to lay off workers will have external effects on the community, not just because laid-off workers have lower purchasing power, but also because the government may have to provide assistance, because it will have lower tax revenue, and because unemployment may lead to social distress. Similarly, on-the-job training is likely to produce benefits external to the firm. Over the long run, as a variety of firms provide training to their workers, the pool of workers with useful skills will be increased. This reduces the cost of hiring and the incidence of any prolonged shortage of specific skills.

The impact of externalities from private labour-market decisions is the most easily understood basis for government intervention in these markets. But the full impact of intervention can only be appreciated when labour-market choices are understood as longer-term investment decisions.

The decision to hire and train workers, or to receive training, is an investment decision because it entails long-term commitments and long-term costs and benefits. An investment in equipment should be made only if the 'present value' of the stream of net benefits over time exceeds the cost of the investment. Similarly, the decision whether or not to hire or to train someone should be based on there being a positive 'present value' of net benefits over the long term.

This capital theory framework highlights a number of points. It makes clear that workers of different age and background present different long-term opportunities and commitments. An older worker may be more experienced, but he also has a shorter working life. A younger worker has a longer working life, but he is also more likely to transfer to another employer, if offered a better compensation package. Also, workers differ vastly in terms of trainability, work ethic, and aptitude. The employer has the difficult task of differentiating workers according to their long-term potential and performance. Finally, employment agreements — the wage profile over time as well as the compensation package — become an important tool to extract the best from the human capital in place, while minimizing the risks of the employer.

Given this, labour market policy, be it minimum wage legislation, unemployment insurance plans, long service pay schemes, wage subsidies, training support, even holiday requirements and employee compensation, has to be considered in the light of its long-term effects. This perspective on policy choices is increasingly relevant to an economy where labour skills have become one of the community's most significant and costly assets. Ensuring adequate investment in skills and maintaining incentives for the efficient use of a highly trained workforce are everywhere a policy priority.

Labour Importation

Hong Kong's labour force growth slowed down markedly in the late 1980s. Meanwhile the economy was growing rapidly, at close to 14 per cent in 1987, for example. Since then the labour force has almost ceased to grow, showing positive growth only in 1991 at a meagre 0.8 per cent. It became apparent that Hong Kong was facing a severe labour shortage with wages rising more rapidly than for many years.

Until the experimental labour importation programme was proposed in 1989, the government had argued that rising real wages were appropriate and would allow labour to share the fruits of economic progress. Under the importation scheme, in order to meet objections from labour, the government mandated that the wages of imported workers must not be lower than the median wages of the corresponding skill categories. Nevertheless, labour groups are quite adamant in their opposition to the labour importation scheme. This opposition has grown as labour-market conditions have become less favourable to local workers.

It is sometimes thought that if wages are allowed to 'clear the market', there can be no labour shortage, since excess demand can be eliminated simply by sufficiently increasing wages. This notion is misguided because eliminating excess demand by raising wages is not the same thing as eliminating a shortage. Even if excess demand is eliminated a shortage can persist in the sense that the prospect of rising wages may stifle risk-averse investments. Excessively high wages may also mean that inputs complementary to labour cannot be put into productive use. In the absence of alternative sources of labour, high wages which eventually render part of the capital stock obsolete are appropriate. On the other hand if labour can be imported much of the otherwise obsolete capital stock can have a much longer economic life.

Quite apart from these considerations, firms that are not sufficiently productive to pay rising wages will be forced to increase their productivity, or they will be driven out of the economy to be replaced by higher value-added enterprises that can survive in a high-wage environment. Firms are more likely to close down if they can set up shop elsewhere in locations offering cheaper labour, and are more likely to shift to higher value-added technologies if they enjoy site-specific advantages that are difficult to replicate elsewhere. Both kinds of adjustment are currently taking place in Hong Kong, and both result in the displacement of traditional workers in manufacturing. But there is no guarantee that the transition will be smooth.

A labour importation scheme can be useful in these circumstances. It is true that unlimited importation of labour at the going 'international' wage rate would dramatically reduce local wages. But government control of labour importation and a suitable levy on imported labour can maintain wages in Hong Kong at levels that slow the exodus of low value-added firms, without reducing the wages of local workers.

At present the Hong Kong government imposes a labour importation levy, and imported workers are supposed to receive a wage equal to the industrial median wage minus the value of the levy. Imported workers cannot change jobs, because their employment visas are issued for specific jobs for specific employers. This means that they are particularly vulnerable to exploitation by their employers. Policing and enforcement are costly. A labour importation levy ranging up to HK$2,500, making it comparable to Singapore's, together with the permission to change jobs, and removal of the minimum wage, would provide better protection for imported workers who in practice are earning wages considerably lower than the official legal wage, and would also provide better protection for local workers who must now compete with them.

Unemployment Protection and Long-service Pay

Hong Kong is noted for its low unemployment rate in a world of persistent high unemployment. It is also noted for the almost complete absence of unemployment protection. In the industrial world, unemployment insurance typically provides the unemployed with 60 per cent or more of their regular earnings (up to a maximum), provided that they have worked in excess of a threshold number of weeks (typically twenty) prior to unemployment.

The system was first introduced in the United States during the Great Depression, and since then has been taken for granted in virtually all industrial nations. Unemployment insurance, however, is known to increase the duration and the incidence of unemployment. Unemployment insurance is also expensive and may force the government into fiscal stress should the insurance premiums collected prove to be inadequate.

In introducing the long-service payment on 1 June 1986, Hong Kong provided, for the first time, a kind of unemployment protection to workers. For any worker who is dismissed for reasons other than disciplinary action, or redundancy, the new provisions required the employer to pay the dismissed worker compensation provided that he meets certain criteria.

To be eligible, a worker must have worked a minimum of five years if he is older than forty-five, and a minimum of ten years if he is younger than forty-one. The compensation is calculated at the rate of two-thirds of the final monthly salary, or wage, for each year of service, up to a maximum of twelve months of salary or HK$180,000, whichever is smaller. When the scheme was first introduced, a discount factor of 25 per cent or 50 per cent on the amount calculated according to the above formula applied to younger workers. The scheme was expanded in 1988 to enable workers to be eligible for the payment when they resign on account of age or ill health. Because these payments are entirely the responsibility of the employer, taxpayers are not burdened at all by the scheme.

As a means to assist temporarily unemployed workers, the long-service payment has both advantages and disadvantages. In several respects it is well designed. It eases the financial strain of the eligible unemployed without encouraging them to be irresponsible. Workers cannot benefit by quitting and then regaining a job after collecting the long-service pay. Workers who intend to take advantage of the long-service payment realize that employers may prefer younger workers, since this reduces the chance of having to bear the long-service payment. Where employers do expect to incur a long-service payment they may offer a lower wage that reflects this obligation. Because long-service pay encourages workers to stay longer with the same employer, employers have a greater incentive to train their workers and develop their skills.

Unfortunately, the scheme is flawed by the effect of the discrete thresholds embodied in it. Firstly, employers have an incentive to lay off workers who are about to become eligible for the benefits. As a result, the payment may be denied to the very people who need it the most. Secondly, the fact that older workers need to work for fewer years to qualify for the payment means that they are less welcomed by employers, unless they can be paid wages lower than those of equivalent younger workers. To the extent that employers do not wish to discriminate openly against older workers by offering lower wages, they may prefer to stipulate age requirements for the job. This reduces the chances of employment for older workers.

Figure 5.1 Maximum Payout Period = Max (4, 4 + 2/5 (age — 30))

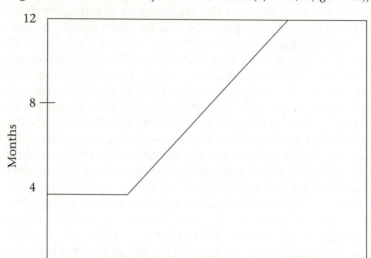

In order to retain the attractive features of the long-service payment while avoiding the undesirable features, I have proposed an 'Earnings Replacement Programme' (ERP). Under the proposed programme, all unemployed people would be entitled to a monthly 'earnings replacement' equal to 75 per cent of monthly earnings prior to unemployment. The payment period is calculated as the product of the 'maximum payout period' and the 'entitlement period ratio' (see Figures 5.1 and 5.2).

The maximum payout period remains flat at four months before the age of 30, but then rises gradually to twelve months by the age of 50. The entitlement period ratio rises from 0 per cent to 100 per cent as 'months employed' rises from 0 to 36 and beyond. Thus a worker who was forty years old, who had been with a company for three years could receive earnings replacement for eight months.

It is also proposed that earnings replacement could be in the form of a loan, or a non-repayable benefit. I have suggested that all payout take the form of loan prior to the age of 30. Beyond the age of 30, however, the earnings replace-

Figure 5.2 Entitlement Period Ratio

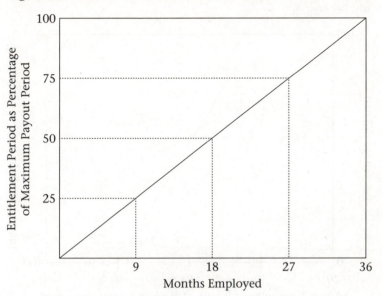

ment would gradually take on a higher proportion of non-repayable benefit, so that by the age of 50 all entitlement would be non-repayable (see Figure 5.3). This feature recognizes that younger workers enjoy more rapidly-rising incomes than older workers, and that they are in a better position to repay loans than older workers. Older workers have a shorter remaining working life, and may have more difficulty in finding a new job.

The scheme is designed so that the requirement that employers pay benefits is not too onerous; also the cost is spread out over a number of months. However, the government might be well advised to require employers to deduct a portion of wages, handing it to the government to be kept as reserve for the ERP. To ensure compliance and expediency, all payments would be centrally administered and paid out by the government from a reserve. Where the benefits are loans, the government would also be responsible for collecting repayments via future employers.

The proposed ERP programme enjoys six advantages. Firstly, it would result in fewer disputes between employers and employees than the current long-service payment scheme.

Figure 5.3 Non-repayable Benefit Ratio = Min (100, 5 × (age — 30)) Per cent

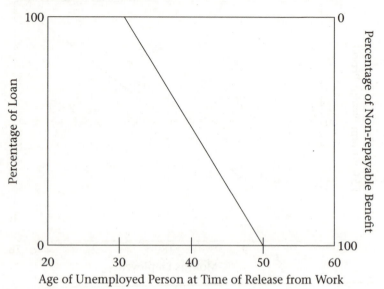

Age of Unemployed Person at Time of Release from Work

Unlike the long-service payment scheme, there are no entitlement thresholds to encourage premature lay-off of workers to avoid the responsibility of having to provide the long-service payment.

Secondly, ERP would not be a burden on the government, because it relies on both loans and private sector support. While administrative cost is a worry, it should be remembered that currently the government is already collecting employment and pay data through the Inland Revenue Department. Recovering loans from workers should not be very difficult. Employers have an incentive to report workers on their payrolls in order to claim deductions and employees must establish a new employment history to be eligible for future benefits.

Thirdly, as Table 5.1 shows, under five scenarios out of nine, the ERP is less costly for employers than the long-service payment. In fact, the effective net cost to employers should be lower than is indicated by the 'burden ratio', since workers aged above 50 would ordinarily be offered a lower starting salary in a new job reflecting the potential cost to employers of

Table 5.1 Comparison of Cost to Employer under ERP and under a 'Streamlined' Version* of the Long-service Payment Scheme

ERP

Age Hired	Age Released	Employment Years	Burden Ratio (Nonrepayable benefit ratio × Months of pay × 3/4) / Months of employment
30	33	3	1.62%
40	43	3	12.48%
50	53	3	25.00%
30	40	10	2.50%
40	50	10	7.50%
50	60	10	7.50%
30	45	15	3.125%
40	55	15	5.00%
50	65	15	5.00%

Long-service Payment Scheme

Age Hired	Age Released	Employment Years	Burden Ratio (Months of pay × 2/3) / Months of employment
30	33	3	5.56%
40	43	3	5.56%
50	53	3	5.56%
30	40	10	5.56%
40	50	10	5.56%
50	60	10	5.56%
30	45	15	5.56%
40	55	15	5.56%
50	65	15	5.56%

* It is assumed that all age and employment period thresholds are removed in the 'Streamlined Version' of the long-service payment scheme.

the ERP. Also employers will have less problem with liquidity because payments are spread out over a number of months.

Fourthly, under the ERP younger workers are given loans rather than non-repayable benefits to help them through a period of unemployment. They therefore have more incentive to look for work than under traditional unemployment schemes. Older workers also have incentive to look for work because, under the proposal, finding a job does not disqualify them for the earnings replacement benefit from their previous employers. New entitlements, however, must be earned afresh from the worker's new employment.

Fifthly, ERP provides the unemployed with 75 per cent of their former purchasing power. It reduces the hardships of the unemployed just as traditional unemployment insurance does.

Finally, like traditional unemployment insurance, the ERP is an 'automatic stabilizer' for the macroeconomy, boosting spending during recessions and widespread unemployment. Although the non-repayable component of the benefit is not a net injection into the economy, the loan component is.

Minimum Wage Legislation

Hong Kong currently imposes a minimum wage for domestic helpers hired from abroad and for foreign workers hired under the labour importation scheme. Otherwise there is no minimum wage legislation. The minimum wages for domestic helpers are set at the government's discretion and for imported workers at the median wage rate for each job category for specific industries. The objective is purportedly to avoid undermining the wage rates for local workers. This is at least in part dictated by the need to pacify local workers who are opposed to the labour importation policy.

Economists usually find minimum wage legislation ineffective as a means to improve the well-being of workers. Firstly, it does not increase the incomes of those whose wages are higher than the minimum wage. For those workers whose wages would have been lower than the statutory minimum wages, only a few will be employed at the minimum wages. The rest will be denied the opportunity of employment altogether. In the industrial world, where minimum wage legislation generally applies, unemployment of unskilled, younger workers, who are supposed to be the major beneficiaries of the legislation, is often serious.

The recent revival of theoretical debate about the impact of minimum wages, and some related US evidence, have underscored the general conclusion that only in quite special circumstances are minimum wages really of benefit to the groups they are designed to help.

With the long-service payment in place, introducing minimum wage legislation would be disastrous for older, unskilled workers. In the absence of minimum wage legislation, the long-service payment may not hurt their employment prospects if wages are flexible. Downward adjustment of wages can then offset the disadvantage of hiring older workers for whom the long-service payment liability is more likely to apply. Introducing a minimum wage will destroy the necessary wage flexibility, thus increasing unemployment among older workers.

As Hong Kong moves towards greater public participation in policy making, pressure is building for more government intervention in the labour market, and minimum wage legislation is no doubt on the agenda of some political parties. If these groups really want to help unskilled workers, they would do better to push the government to find ways to improve the employability of the unskilled workers. Better retraining is one way forward.

There are also two other ways of assisting low-skill, low-wage workers — the negative income tax and the universal wage subsidy scheme. The negative income tax was first suggested by Milton Friedman. The basic idea is to provide a universal taxable transfer to households. This scheme has found favour among economists. The universal wage subsidy is a similar idea, but is conditional on the employment status of those assisted.

Although it has not been tried elsewhere, a universal wage subsidy scheme is easy to implement and should be effective in improving the welfare of low-skilled workers. The idea is to provide a lump sum, taxable wage supplement to all workers working in excess of thirty hours a week. Together with a higher standard tax rate (say raising it from 15 per cent to 17 per cent), or perhaps with the abolition of the standard tax rate so that high-income people will be subject to a higher marginal tax rate, this supplement would have a net redistributive effect among the employed in favour of the low-wage workers.

Like the minimum wage the universal wage subsidy ensures an effective 'minimum wage' for workers. Yet unlike the legal minimum wage the universal wage subsidy does not set a floor to market wages. At the same time this scheme is superior to the negative income tax proposal of Milton Friedman. A negative income tax redistributes income from income-earning people to non-income-earning people. This clearly has adverse incentive effects.

Some people may be concerned that a wage subsidy scheme opens up opportunities for fraud. To implement the scheme the government needs to have a record of each worker employed in excess of 30 hours. Information about every worker has to be filed by the employer with the government in order for the wage supplement to be paid. It may be objected that the employer may collaborate with individuals who pretend to be working in order to share the wage supplements. It may also be objected that the employer may reduce the wage offered in view of the supplement.

With regard to the first objection, occasional random checking by inspectors plus a stiff penalty should be sufficient to rule out large-scale fraud. With regard to the second objection, it should be noted that employers have to compete for workers in the marketplace. The uniform wage supplement will not give any one employer an edge over the others. Competition will leave relative wages more or less intact, with the result that low-income workers benefit.

Wage Subsidies for Disadvantaged Workers

Hong Kong is presently in the process of structural adjustment resulting from its changing comparative advantage vis-à-vis other countries. Labour cost and land cost are climbing, making it increasingly unattractive as a location for standardized manufacturing. Meanwhile Hong Kong is increasingly important as an intermediary between China and foreign markets and investors, and as a source of both capital and ideas. This economic restructuring is reducing jobs rapidly in some sectors.

Economic restructuring is leaving many older workers, whose skills have become obsolete, out in the cold. The government has considered setting up a retraining programme for the disadvantaged as a means of helping them to resecure jobs. This may not be cost effective, because their remaining working life is relatively short, while acquiring a new skill from scratch at that age is difficult, especially for those with a limited educational background.

Unable to find alternative employment at a market wage, many workers give up looking for work altogether. There is little doubt that these workers face tremendous hardships and eventually have to rely on public assistance. Providing a wage subsidy for these workers will increase the attractiveness of hiring them. A wage subsidy may actually save money, because there will less demand for public assistance. The wage subsidy will allow them to continue as productive members of the community more effectively than additional training.

Training

Training is an activity that yields private benefits to both the trainee and the employer. It should be left to the market if these private benefits account for all the marginal benefits to society. In general training can be regarded as a form of investment in human capital. The trainee benefits because his productivity and his income rises with the new skills acquired. The employer benefits because, notwithstanding the higher wages paid, higher profits can be expected because of higher overall productivity.

The increase in productivity also benefits consumers, but this presents no ground for government subsidy. This 'external benefit' occurs through the price mechanism. As productivity increases and costs fall, as long as there is sufficient competition, this is reflected in lower market prices.

However, training does produce two other kinds of externality which justify some form of public support. Firstly, the skills imparted potentially benefit employers who do not pay for the training. These employers can simply hire the worker and benefit from the new skills he has acquired. Even if they do not actually hire these workers right away, the availability of a variety of different skills in the marketplace reduces the risks of firms being caught short of particular skills and improves the investment environment. This is particularly true for skills that are not firm-specific. In practice there are very few skills that are entirely firm-specific. So the external benefits may be significant.

To support the development of non-firm-specific skills, the Vocational Training Council, set up in 1982, runs a number of technical institutes and training centres offering courses for skilled workers, draughtsmen, technicians, and apprentices. The training programmes are directly tuned in to the needs of industry.

Secondly, socially valuable, but commercially less valuable skills require subsidy, because the trainee cannot capture sufficient benefits of the training in the marketplace to offset his opportunity costs. The skills of scientists who do basic research are a case in point. Government support for postgraduate programmes in our tertiary institutions is justified on this ground. In general, a postgraduate qualification does not raise incomes sufficiently to justify the huge costs incurred by the institutions as well as by the individual in his long years of studies. To the extent, however, that society benefits by high quality research, the investment is justified.

Recently, in response to the continued industrial restructuring in Hong Kong and the migration of production plants to China, the government started a new initiative to re-equip workers with new skills. This effort is justified by the perceived external diseconomy of a growing number of dislocated and disadvantaged workers whose skills have been rendered obsolete by ongoing industrial restructuring.

This responsibility now rests with the Employees Retraining Board (ERB), a statutory body established under the Employees Training Ordinance on 16 October 1992. The Board is financed by a levy on imported workers paid in a lump sum by the employer upon initial approval of the application for the allotment of the required quota. These funds are pooled in the Employees Retraining Fund and earmarked for training purposes.

The retraining courses can be divided into four types:

1. Skill training. These are full-time programmes with a duration of four to six weeks. Trainees are given a monthly allowance, currently of HK$3,400.

2. Job hunting skill courses. These last for one week. An allowance, currently of HK$800, is provided.
3. Evening basic courses on languages and computers. An allowance of HK$30 per evening is given.
4. Skill upgrading courses for to-be-dislocated workers. These are preventive in nature, designed to allow workers to keep their jobs in a changing environment.

According to Chow Tung Shan, Executive Director of the Employees Retraining Board, the programmes administered by the ERB have gone through two phases and are in the process of going into the third and fourth phases. The first phase was entirely aimed at providing displaced, unemployed workers with new skills to enable them to seek alternative employment. This was found to be costly and not very effective. The second phase was aimed at building on the old skills of the displaced workers and the objective was to increase their productivity so that they can become employable again. The third phase was preventive in nature, aimed at workers at risk of losing their jobs because of obsolescence of their skills. An example is the retraining of draughtsmen in computer-aided design. The Employees Retraining Board has also been given the new mission of retraining disadvantaged workers — namely victims of industrial accidents and elderly and disabled workers — to become employable again.

Unfortunately, for elderly, poorly educated workers retraining is likely to be costly and ineffective. Wage subsidies that are designed to increase the attractiveness of hiring these workers should be seriously considered. Such subsidies would allow these workers to remain productive and thus enhance their morale. Even though their productivity may be lower than the subsidized wage, the subsidy will be worth the cost if it is cheaper than the cost of retraining, especially when the benefit of the retraining is in doubt. Also, the subsidy may be cheaper than the cost of public assistance otherwise required when workers suffer prolonged unemployment.

Labour Relations

A harmonious relationship between employers and employees is important both for economic growth and for social stability. However, in an industrial society occasional conflicts between capital and labour are unavoidable. When there are disputes, it is common for labour unions to resort to strikes as a means of pressing their case. Early in 1993, the stewardesses of Cathay Pacific Airlines engaged in unprecedented strike action that caused much confusion and havoc for the travelling public. The action ended largely as a result of exhaustion and financial stress on the part of the striking workers, and the softening of the position of the employer as it incurred losses, both financially and in terms of public image.

While it was the pain borne by the employees and the employer that finally put an end to the strike, the pain borne by third parties, namely the travelling public and their associates, was a totally unnecessary by-product. There is little doubt that if both parties had felt the pain earlier they would have resolved their dispute sooner, reducing the external cost imposed on the public.

In industrial countries certain occupations are often forbidden to take strike action because a strike is thought to cause too much social loss. From an analytical point of view, however, there is no conceptual difference between a strike by the medical profession and a strike by garbage collectors. Any difference is just a matter of the seriousness of the external loss. In principle, then, imposing a 'strike tax' on both parties at the bargaining table for causing inconvenience to the public is a better, fairer solution.

The strike tax only needs to correspond to the estimated external loss. On the reasonable assumption that the external loss increases with the duration of the strike, the tax should rise over time. The tax should be based on man-days of the strike action and shared by both capital and labour. Ideally, it should be used to alleviate the losses imposed on the innocent public. A labour union which has a justified, strong grievance might win sufficient public support to fund a prolonged strike. For obvious reasons a strike tax would be unpopular with labour unions, but so is a 'back-to-work order' imposed by the government, or laws banning certain kinds of strikes altogether.

The fact is that as the economy gets more and more sophisticated and more interdependent the economic cost of strikes will be greater and greater. The right to strike, traditionally regarded as sacrosanct, should be looked at more critically. Taking a balanced view and looking at the costs and benefits, rather than banning strikes altogether or taking a *laissez-faire* attitude to them, we should tax both employers and employees for the disruption that strikes cause upon the economy.

Understandably, labour unions in Hong Kong have been pressing for entrenchment of the right to strike through new laws prohibiting the dismissal of workers on 'unfair' grounds. It is not obvious that this kind of legislation will benefit labour. In general, the more difficult it is for employers to dismiss workers, the more unattractive it is for them to hire workers in the first place. The unemployment rate of Hong Kong has been uncharacteristically low in a world of high unemployment. This may well change should legislation against unfair dismissal be passed in Hong Kong.

We have examined a range of labour market policies in the light of the theory of externality and cost/benefit analysis. The conclusion that emerges is that government intervention often has long-term effects on incentives. Policies with the best of intentions may turn out to have adverse effects on the groups who are supposed to benefit.

The minimum wage is a case in point, hurting underprivileged people by depriving them of the chance to secure jobs. The long-service payment is intended to help the elderly, but it may discourage employers from hiring them. Policies making it difficult to fire workers also discourage hiring. The Hong Kong government has been steadfast in its resistance to introducing a minimum wage in Hong Kong, with the exception of imported workers. But as the legislature becomes more and more responsive to the demands of the electorate, Hong Kong may be more ready to introduce economically irrational policies.

On the other hand, while bad policies can backfire, less traditional, but well-designed policies can help the underprivileged. A wage subsidy will give the low-skilled, poorly prepared workers a better chance to get jobs than will training. Training should be reserved for those who are more likely to benefit from it. A universal wage subsidy combined with a more progressive income tax system can achieve higher incomes for the low-skilled without putting their jobs at risk. The strike tax proposed will not be politically popular, but as the economy becomes more and more interdependent it will become more and more valuable as a means to reduce the disruptions that are bound to occur. The evolution of Hong Kong's labour market policies will require much leadership and courage, and above all, enlightened economic thinking.

6. Protecting Hong Kong Consumers

Pamela Chan Wong Shui

D18

Caveat Emptor?

It has been argued that the government should not devote public resources to consumer protection laws and measures because consumers are victims of their own stupidity and greed; *caveat emptor*, i.e. 'let the buyer beware' should suffice. This view fails to recognize the imbalance of power that exists between the individual consumer and business.

Even in the best of circumstances, there is an imbalance of power between business and consumers. Traders, whether large or small, have greater resources than an individual consumer. Businesses are more organized and have access to expert advice in order to protect their interests.

In seeking redress, consumers have to assess carefully whether the outcome justifies the action. When determined customers fight an unreasonable exemption clause in a service agreement, they may have to take the matter to court. The time spent and costs incurred, even at the complaint stage, are daunting, not to mention litigation expenses. On the other hand traders are less disadvantaged. In the first instance, the terms of the service agreement drafted by traders are likely to be in their favour. In litigation, they are also assisted by abundant legal and expert advice. Finally, the cost of litigation is met from the company's coffers, but is ultimately passed on to other customers through increases in the price of goods or services.

This situation has been made more difficult by technological developments that have produced a stream of new products and sophisticated services. Consumers can no longer compare products from their appearance alone. Quality is not readily discernible at the time of purchase. Ingredients or materials used may have harmful long-term effects on consumers and the environment. As services become more specialized, e.g. medical and legal services, consumers encounter greater difficulty in comparing their quality and value for money.

Change of Government Policy

Governor Christopher Patten's 1992 policy address to the Legislative Council sent a clear message that the *laissez-faire* or 'positive non-intervention' doctrines, which have been the cornerstone of Hong Kong's approach to consumer protection for many years, can no longer apply in an increasingly competitive world market and in the face of structural changes in the economy. To sustain the economic growth of Hong Kong, he argued, goods and services must be competitive 'within a sound, fair framework of regulation and law'.

He further affirmed that where monopolies are unavoidable, the government has a duty to act in defence of the public interest through controls on profits or prices. The Consumer Council was called upon to join forces with the government to defend free markets and to give consumers redress against unscrupulous business practices.

This policy change is long overdue. It is in line with growing consumer expectations, expectations that are the result of a number of new developments. Firstly, there have been changes in the political arena. Direct election and a more open attitude by the administration in explaining its policies have encouraged the population not to accept matters as they are. More questions are being asked and the public demands accountability from politicians and the government. Consumer issues attract wide attention.

Secondly, the increase in real per capita income of the population has produced both an 'income effect' and a 'substitution effect' — a shift in demand from relatively inferior goods to more sophisticated services. Consumers would rather pay more for quality products than put up with hazardous goods. They shun shoddy services and defy unfair contract terms, hence the enactment of product safety laws. New laws to control exemption clauses and unfair contract terms have been endorsed by the Legislative Council with little opposition. In addition, the legislature also supported moves to licence insurance intermediaries, travel agents, and estate agents.

The following are notable milestones:

1. Control of Exemption Clauses Ordinance (enacted in 1989 and came into effect in December 1990, limiting the ability of sellers to create exemption from liability).
2. Pesticides Ordinance (amendments in 1990 to extend safety standards to domestic pesticides, i.e. mosquito spray etc.).
3. Gas Safety Ordinance (commenced 1 April 1991 to regulate the safety of domestic gas appliances).
4. Electricity Ordinance (commenced 15 November 1991 to regulate the safety of domestic electrical appliances).
5. Consumer Council Ordinance (amendments in 1992 and 1994, to extend the remit of the Council).
6. Toys and Children's Products Safety Ordinance (commenced 1 July 1993 to provide for safety standards for toys and specified children's products).
7. Travel Agents Ordinance (amendments in 1992, 1993, and 1994, to provide for greater protection for clients).
8. Consumer Goods Safety Ordinance (enacted in 1994 to regulate the safety of consumer goods not covered by existing legislation).
9. Amendments to Sales of Goods Ordinance, 1994 (to set out obligations of a seller to supply goods of merchantible quality and reasonably fit for their purpose) and Supply of Services (Implied Terms) Ordinance (to specify that services must be supplied with reasonable care and skill and within a reasonable time).
10. Unconscionable Contracts Ordinance, 1994 (to control unconscionable terms in consumer contracts).
11. Information Disclosure by property developers, 1991. (The consent letter issued by the government to approve pre-sale of uncompleted properties now requires developers to disclose information on units in uncompleted buildings. A detailed sales brochure and price list must be available seven days and three days respectively prior to sale).
12. Deregulation of interest rates in phases and disclosure of information from the banking sector, 1994.
13. Self-regulation of insurance intermediaries, 1993.
14. Establishment of Consumer Legal Action Fund (to assist consumers in pursuit of legal justice, 1994).

Challenges in the New Economy

Despite these important achievements, there is still much to be done. The agenda for change is being set by new forces at work in the Hong Kong economy. Three features of economic development are important. Firstly, there is emerging concern with regard to the market power of large corporations, including so called 'natural monopolies' (i.e. economic sectors such as water supply where it is efficient to have only one supplier). Related to this is concern about the terms of the provision of services to consumers by large scale public agencies. Secondly, Hong Kong's consumers are witnessing a significant technological advance, especially in telecommunication, broadcasting, and information technology. While we are sure to derive benefits from this process, it raises new concerns about the protection of consumer interests. Thirdly, the economic future presents a more uncertain picture, as the structural change in the local economy is caught in the cross current of a slowdown in China's economic cycle.

Market Power and Competition

Rapid economic integration with China has accelerated the structural transformation process in Hong Kong's domestic market. Due to lower land and labour costs, Hong Kong's entrepreneurs have relocated their manufacturing activities to China. As a result, Hong Kong has evolved from a manufacturing-based to a service-based economy. While a manufacturing, export-oriented economy is more attuned to competition in the international market, the service-based economy of 'non-tradable' products is susceptible to a higher concentration of market power.

Huge companies with potential market power have emerged already in Hong Kong, in part as a result of deliberate government policy. The two supermarket chains, 'Welcome' and 'Park 'n Shop', together claim 70 per cent of the total market share. With legal, cultural, and technical factors restricting competition, the local gas supplier will continue to expand its market share well above the current level of 51 per cent.

To regulate utilities and franchised companies such as bus and telephone companies, the government has relied for many years on the 'maximum permissible profits rule', i.e. a maximum 15 per cent of the rate of return on capital investment. This form of regulation has led to criticism that the regulated companies are given an incentive to over-capitalize, i.e. to increase their asset base to justify larger profits. Also, this regulatory regime exerts no pressure on companies to minimize cost and operate efficiently.

In 1993, when the government reviewed the franchise for Hong Kong Telecom International Ltd., the mode of regulation was changed from setting the maximum rate of profit to establishing a 'price-cap' i.e. setting a ceiling for price increases at the rate of inflation less 'x' per cent.

The Office of the Telecommunications Authority (OFTA), the regulator, will now need to examine whether the price-cap formula adopted, in particular, the 4 per cent 'x' factor, is equitable for the company and consumers. Also, with the benefit of experience, it should review the impact of other competition-enhancing measures.

The government must also review its arrangements with other franchised companies, including the two power companies and bus companies.

Increasingly, regulators in advanced economies have come to recognize the advantage of inducing competition rather than regulating. Governments have been attempting to remove barriers to entry for new competitors. In the cases of the gas supply and telecommunication industries, the dominant supplier can be asked to separate its network operation from its role as a service provider so that new competitors can access the market without having to incur heavy investments in set-up costs. In return, the network provider is suitably compensated for the use of its facility. In the United States, the United Kingdom, and Australia, there has been great enhancement in consumer benefit from this development in terms of lower prices and increased choices as markets become competitive.

Hong Kong has followed this practice in the telecommunication industry. Hong Kong Telecom has opened up its network to three Fixed Telecommunications Network Service (FTNS) operators. Competition pressure forced down prices for international calls, bringing immediate substantial benefit to consumers. Separately, the government is looking at a proposal to open up the gas distribution network to become a 'common carrier' for new entrants, but rejected the proposal to subject the dominant gas supplier, Hong Kong and China Gas Co. Ltd., to price cap regulation. The ultimate decision will reveal how far government is willing to go in dealing with these 'natural' monopolies.

The government should also consider the advantages of designating one regulator for each industry, or employing one regulator for similar types of utilities, for example an Energy Commission responsible for regulating the electricity and gas companies.

Regulation should always be in the public interest, but regulators should be expected to explain openly the yardstick by which they measure the performance of those regulated. For example, this yardstick might include issues of universal access, affordability, or environmental benefit, in addition to the issues of quality and price.

Public Sector Services

Another issue gaining prominence is the balance between the public and private sectors in the health care and housing markets. In addition to the complex issues of social policy and public finance raised by these areas of government activity, there is concern over the dominance of the public sector in the provision of health and housing services.

The effort by the Hospital Authority (HA), an umbrella body of forty-two health-care institutions employing over 38,000 medical practitioners, to improve its services to the public has created a sizable shift of patients from the private sector to the public sector. The market share of the Hospital Authority by patient days has risen from 90 per cent in 1991 (pre-HA) to 92 per cent in 1994.

Similar concerns may arise regarding the share of public housing *vis-à-vis* the private market. Over 50 per cent of Hong Kong's population live in public housing at subsidized rentals or at much below market price for purchased, public flats.

While the public sector can perform a crucial function by creating healthy competition with the private sector so that there is more choice and better quality services (health care) and products (properties) at affordable cost, monitoring government departments and agencies is a legitimate public concern.

Some progress has been made. Government departments have been asked to make performance pledges to members of the public and be assessed against performance indicators. The Bill of Rights, the Information Ordinance, and the Commissioner for Administrative Complaints (COMAC) are effective instruments for ensuring that the conduct of business by government departments is within their proper scope and is 'transparent'. This momentum should be maintained, even as the political situation alters.

In the past few years, we have witnessed a change in the hospital/patient relationship. The proclamation of the Patients Rights Charter by the Hospital Authority and the Hong Kong Medical Association and the effort of the former to cultivate a culture change contributed to this transformation process. Patients can hope for an increasingly client-oriented health care provider.

Meanwhile, there have been steps by some groups in the public housing estates to assert their rights as tenants rather than remain passive recipients of housing-welfare benefits.

The government now needs to examine the operation of the Water Authority, Postal Service, and Company and Land Registries. The Company Registry and Lands Registry are now operating on a trading-fund basis, inducing them to operate more like private businesses. The Post Office is soon to follow suit. Policy makers will have to face up to the question of whether these departments should be privatized and if so, what will be the effect of privatization on consumer interests.

Creating a Competitive Market Place

Hong Kong is probably the only advanced economy that has not enacted a competition law to confront possible abuse of market power. Consumer protection laws also lag behind and are inadequate in dealing with anti-competitive market practices. Tie-in sales, exclusive dealings, predatory pricing, and price-fixing are tolerated as a matter of course in business transactions. Examples are abundant; they include the scale charge for conveyancing and the Interest Rate Rule of the Hong Kong Association of Banks.

The need to establish a comprehensive competition policy involving fair-trading legislation to cover all business sectors has been the subject of keen debate. Supporters contend that Hong Kong, ranked as the world's third most competitive economy in the *World Economic Forum 1995 Report*, should not refrain from setting up a comprehensive legal structure to ensure that a free market exists for all players. They note that international institutions like the Organisation for Economic Co-operation and Development (OECD), United Nations Conference on Trade and Development (UNCTAD), and World Trade Organisation (WTO) have domestic competition law and international competition firmly on their agenda.

As international fair-trade expert Frederic Jenny remarks, 'competition law is, and should be seen as, an integral part of the development of a modern market economy. Every developed economy has fair trading laws and an increasing number of developing countries are following suit. Hong Kong cannot afford to be left out in this process. Japan, Korea, India, Nepal, and Taiwan have already enacted Competition and Fair Trading Laws.' Closer to home, China enacted fair trading laws on 1 December 1993 and is currently contemplating a competition law.

So far the government has adopted a case-by-case approach to promoting greater competition. Following a 1994 Consumer Council report on the interest rate cartel administered by the Hong Kong Association of Banks for forty years, the government has liberalized interest rates for deposits of seven days and over, but has postponed further liberalization. As noted above, the telecommunication market was deregulated in July 1995 allowing three new fixed network operators to compete directly with Hong Kong Telecom, breaking up the latter's monopoly franchise of over a century. Likewise, more participants in the broadcasting industry are anticipated by 1998, as the exclusive rights of the cable television licence expire and new entrants compete against two terrestrial, satellite, and the incumbent cable operator.

The government also seized the opportunity of licence review for ATV, TVB, Commercial Radio, Star TV, and Hong Kong Telecom to insert new provisions in the licences to ensure competition and fair dealings among licensees.

While such initiatives from the government are welcomed, a comprehensive competition framework remains one of the most important contributions that the government could make in supporting the economy of Hong Kong in the new circumstances. The government must be mindful of the fact that effective competition not only safeguards consumer interest by ensuring a level playing field but competition and fair trading laws benefit consumers as well as business.

Concern over the cost of enacting and implementing competition and fair trading laws is legitimate, but it may be more costly to devise sector-specific rules than to take a comprehensive approach. Moreover, although setting up an enforcement agency like the Office of Fair Trading in the United Kingdom does incur costs, the absence of such an agency is also costly, the cost of subjecting consumers and sectors of business to undesirable consequences of restrictive practices and monopolistic abuses.

Consumer Policies and Consumption Law

The needs of the more affluent, sophisticated consumer differ significantly from those of the economically disadvantaged urban poor. Consequently, a wide range of legal protection catering for these distinct needs is required.

Given this, Hong Kong must provide for both 'consumption laws' and 'consumer laws'. 'Consumption laws' seek to recognize the basic needs of people and to protect those who are discriminated against and find themselves in a dependent position in sellers' markets. 'Consumer laws' address the desire for information, choice, and value for money typical of better off consumers in a buyers' market.

The basic needs normally protected by 'consumption laws' are not confined to survival needs alone e.g. clean water or basic food. It includes curbing so-called 'unconscionableness' in contracts and other consumer credit issues. The distributive justice angle to consumer protection has been the subject of active debate in some advanced economies. The issues include equal access to consumption opportunities and access for the poor and disadvantaged to rights of enforcement.

For example, a new 'need concept' in contract law has emerged in Germany, postulating a 'social interpretation' of contract law to provide for a 'social *force majeure*' remedy. In essence, when a consumer encounters great difficulty due to unemployment, illness, or divorce and is unable to meet contractual obligations previously entered into freely, the court may intervene and alter the contract so that it is equitable and remains fair. In Australia, following a public outcry against banking institutions which had been forcing out unprofitable customers, the Price Surveillance Authority is looking into the price of banking service charges.

Despite Hong Kong's position as one of the world's largest financial centres, Hong Kong does not have a consumer credit law. Also, measures to safeguard consumers confronting the wide array of financial products are in their infancy, to the extent that they exist at all. In establishing such laws, Hong Kong must be prepared to confront the differences in the ethical versus the market-based issues in consumer protection.

Equally, Hong Kong must gear up its 'consumer laws' to face up to new challenges. Hong Kong is heading for the information superhighway. It has the world's first fully digitalized telephone system and the most comprehensive optical fibre network. With this infrastructure in place, it has proceeded to experiment with a video-on-demand service. The adult population is accustomed to using cash dispenser machines, and awaits with interest the arrival of the 'smart' card and the cashless society.

It is not possible to anticipate all the issues that new products and new shopping technologies will create for consumer interests. However, consumer policies and laws should observe two principles. Firstly, consumer interest should be high on the agenda in the system design of the new products and services. Innovations increasing efficiency and convenience should not be achieved at the expense of the uninformed consumer. Affected parties should be fully consulted so that they will be aware of any detrimental consequences of a choice. For example, the Central Clearing and Settlement System (CCASS) for stocks and shares greatly enhanced market efficiency, benefiting big corporate dealers and brokers, but the scriptless system caused great inconvenience to some small purchasers, leaving them open to higher brokerage charges. Likewise, the proposed conversion of the existing land registration system to a title registration system is weighted heavily in favour of protecting the purchaser.

Secondly, consumer benefit from technological developments should be maximized. At the user level, full regard should be given to users' convenience and protection as technology advances. For instance, the government should encourage initiatives to devise standardized encryption and decoding methods so that users need not install several different systems. Resources can be saved with better co-ordination and foresight. In so doing, government must address the concern that standardization may impede technological innovation, suppress competition, and cause privacy problems.

To ensure that regulatory policies are keeping abreast with rapid developments and to provide for a level playing field for all market participants is no easy task. The formation of legislative and/or regulatory standards takes time. Success requires proactive initiatives from government officials equipped with the necessary expertise.

A current issue is the extension of Hong Kong Telecom's permission to offer video-on-demand service upon conclusion of their pilot run. The government proposes to lift the ban on Hong Kong Telecom from taking part in the pay-television market. In these circumstances, will Hong Kong Telecom's market power as provider of an international telecommunication service, a local fixed network telecom service, mobile phones, and video-on-demand be too great?

Co-operation and Harmonization with Neighbouring Economies

Hong Kong's integration with the China market has accelerated. As more products move across the border in both directions, product quality, warranties, and after-sales service call for closer co-operation between producers, manufacturers, regulatory authorities, and consumer organizations in Hong Kong and China. Closer alignment of product standards is essential if undesirable consequences are to be avoided. For example, vegetables from China may occasionally contain harmful pesticides, or unsafe products from Hong Kong may be dumped in China as Hong Kong tightens controls over toys and other general consumer products.

The same is true for Hong Kong's relations with other economies in the region. Hong Kong must speak up to ensure that adequate safeguards for consumer interest are in place in domestic markets and in cross-border activities and to prevent an influx of unwanted, substandard goods, or even fraudulent and unethical services from other countries.

Consumer protection and the issue of redress become more complicated as companies become increasingly global in scope, since most activities of governments are limited by the borders. Pursuit of legal justice outside their own jurisdiction is a task beyond the reach of the consumer. Governments and consumer groups in the region must work hand in hand to promote good business conduct and to stamp out abusive practices.

Consumer Empowerment

The ultimate defenders of consumer interests are of course consumers themselves. Consumers should be encouraged to take action to defend their rights rather than passively accepting what traders are willing to give them, or what the consumer bodies successfully obtain for them. This means giving consumers more information and training to develop personal consumer skills. Experience has shown that consumers do take heed of the findings relating to products tested through independent laboratories. Higher-quality products move quickly off retail shelves, while the sales of products identified as inferior plummet.

Consumers' interests are often diffuse, yet collectively they are capable of exerting pressure on manufacturers and retailers. For example, consumers in Taiwan have been successful in boycotts against airlines and even government authorities. In Hong Kong, there is a welcome trend toward the formation of concern groups expressing opinions on transport policy, the practices of travel agents, and other issues.

There are now more channels open for consumer action, including the Consumer Council, COMAC, Legislative Council, and the media. In future there will be increasing calls on the Consumer Legal Action Fund (CLAF) for assistance from groups of consumers who have suffered from business malpractice.

Big corporations also see the need to involve, rather than alienate, their customers. Firms have been setting up consumer consultative groups. Despite some initial reluctance and scepticism, many corporations are now convinced that they benefit from open and direct communication with their customers.

Hong Kong is experiencing exciting changes in the political and economic arena. Amidst optimism that Hong Kong's economy will remain active and prosperous, we must remember that the market is for the people and not the other way around. Consumer sovereignty and economic efficiency can be attained with the joint help of competition policy and consumer protection laws. At the same time, the right balance must be found between government regulation and industry self-regulation in monitoring franchises, professional and occupational groups, and other legal limitations on competition. Hong Kong also needs to keep its consumer protection legislation in line with international standards.

There is no cause for fear that Hong Kong will over-legislate to protect its consumers. Hong Kong is proud of its pragmatism. We should certainly be able to avoid the pitfalls experienced by other jurisdictions.

Ralph Nader, in his keynote address delivered at the 13th World Congress of the International Organisation of Consumers Unions held in Hong Kong in July 1991, noted that 'a more comprehensive world view of a consumer-sovereign economic system will begin to emerge to shape technology, government policies and the business practices of the future'. Governments and business, he argued, 'will have to heed first and foremost the priorities of consumer well-being and respect for future generations.' In this larger context, everybody in the community is a consumer, including those in business.

7. Housing: Getting the Priorities Right

Chris Blundell

Housing a population in excess of six million in a built-up residential area of only fifty square kilometres makes Hong Kong one of the world's most densely populated urban environments. The terrain, limited land supply, high land prices, and the locational preferences of the populace all conspire to create this dense urban environment on expensive land. The economics of real estate further require that the most intensive form of development should be adopted, namely high-rise, flatted blocks.

In the public sector these pressures have resulted in a massive stock of (by international standards) generally small and low quality dwellings, although this is gradually changing with the latest generation of Harmony blocks, which are more spacious for residents. Management is professional, although cost containment pressures result in basic standards of service.

Developments in the private sector, by their very nature, create a mixture of individually owned and collectively managed property. Not all owners are interested in, or are able to afford, adequate standards of management and maintenance of their property. In these circumstances, there is an increased probability of poor standards of management and maintenance of the physical infrastructure, particularly in older private sector developments.

Periods of high and sustained economic growth over the last ten years have inevitably changed the housing standards, and expectations, of many sections of the Hong Kong public, in particular the new middle classes. Others who have been less fortunate are looking for a flow of 'trickle down' benefits from this transformation. Hong Kong is not, and probably never will be, a welfare state in the Western sense, but the incongruity of a strongly performing economy and rising middle-class wealth on one side, and poor housing conditions on the other, reinforces demands for better housing. How should government respond to these problems in formulating and managing housing policy in the territory?

Hong Kong's Unique Housing Markets

Given the government's predisposition to market-oriented solutions, housing policy might be expected to stress increased home ownership and minimal intervention in the market. In practice, Hong Kong has developed a mixed economy of housing in which the state sector plays a significant part with 46 per cent of dwellings provided through the Hong Kong Housing Authority ('the Authority') and the Hong Kong Housing Society ('the Society'). Out of a permanent dwelling stock of 1,867,000; some 685,000 (35.6 per cent) are within the public rented sector, including the rental stock of the Society; 994,000 (53.2 per cent) are within the private sector; and a further 187,000 dwellings (10.0 per cent) are within the Authority's Home Ownership Scheme.

Housing in Hong Kong is a major public service with 2.36 million persons living in public rental dwellings and an estimated further 567,000 persons living in home ownership dwellings developed by the Authority. The Authority itself is a large and financially autonomous body with an annual turnover of approximately HK$28 billion, comprising about 10.5 per cent of public sector expenditure, and employing 14,000 staff. An additional 35,000–45,000 new dwellings (rental and home ownership) are produced and over 40,000 rental flats allocated each year. Added to this, there is the substantial task of providing housing for the 150,000 households languishing on the waiting list and the redevelopment of significant numbers of older housing blocks with the attendant rehousing obligations. Intervention on this scale is testimony to the importance of housing and suggests government acknowledgement that it cannot simply leave things to the market.

It is undoubtedly true that the housing markets in recent years have been under considerable stress. Demand has grown rapidly as a consequence of three factors: the booming economy of southern China and its impact on Hong Kong incomes; the effect of negative real interest rates due to high local inflation and low US interest rates affecting Hong Kong through the linked exchange rate mechanism; and the clearing of political obstacles to the development of the Territory. In these circumstances, much has been made of the problem of affordability of home ownership for Hong Kong's new middle classes.

The affordability of home ownership is also an important policy issue given the need for the 'filtering' of rental dwellings to take place whereby better-off tenants trade up from renting to ownership, releasing a flow of dwellings for re-letting to lower income households. This process has the twin advantages of making the most effective use of the stock of public rental dwellings in housing those in greatest need, and more effectively targeting the subsidy involved in supplying such dwellings. The affordability of home ownership thus deserves serious consideration in any comprehensive housing policy. Whether it should be given the prominence it currently receives in housing policy debates is open to question.

Some seek a solution to housing problems in market-oriented policy. Local economists Richard Wong and S. Staley, for example, have argued forcefully for rolling back government involvement in housing provision through, *inter alia*, substantial privatization of public rental housing (without resale restrictions), abolition of rent controls for the private rented sector, and a wholly *laissez-faire* policy toward the operation of the private market for dwellings for sale. Other commentators, L. W. C. Lai, for example, similarly argue for less political intervention in the operation of Hong Kong's housing markets, although they support the stimulation of additional supply (i.e. a market-based stimulus) and effective use of the planning and land control system.

It is commonly held that rent controls act as a disincentive to the private market since landlords are forced to accept unrealistically low, or even negative, rates of return on their investment, resulting in a reduction in the supply of new dwellings for rent and in the quality of dwellings already available.

Some of the earlier controls on rents in the private sector, particularly those affecting pre-war tenancies, were clearly out of date, but severe shortages of supply, and low wage levels relative to the cost of providing housing put tenants at a decided disadvantage. Far from being the underdog, landlords now command considerable power. In seeking to ensure effective market operation, the pernicious effects of unrestrained landlordism do need to be checked. Recent evidence suggests that 'soft' or 'second generation' rent controls may provide an answer. These restrain market forces by, for example, formulae-driven increases, but achieve some mitigation for tenants without so penalizing landlords that disincentives to supply and maintenance set in.

The second argument advanced in support of less government involvement is that the provision of public rental accommodation has little effect on the consumption of housing, but acts primarily to reduce the cost to the tenant. Current evidence from recent lettings to public rental tenants in Hong Kong suggests that this is not the case. A Housing Authority survey (September 1994) of new lettings of public rental housing showed that 80 per cent of respondents reported an improvement in living conditions, of whom 77 per cent were now living in larger flats (the average living space having increased from 4.7 square metres to 9.2 square metres per person), while 30 per cent had previously occupied non-self-contained or temporary structures. The median monthly rent was HK$960, representing a rent-to-income ratio of 8.2 per cent, compared to a previous median rent of HK$3,100 and rent-to-income ratio of 23.3 per cent for those rehoused from private rented housing. The median monthly income for those having occupied public rental housing for only one to two years was about HK$8,000 compared to a median income for Hong Kong as a whole of HK$14,500. Table 7.1 below provides this information over a slightly longer timescale. While the data covers larger population groups (i.e. all public sector tenants and private sector tenants and not simply low income households seeking public housing) it does confirm the overall picture.

These figures confirm the real value of public housing, particularly for lower income households, and the improvement in living standards (as measured in space and self-containment) that commonly takes place, in addition to the reduction of housing costs (an important concession to households on such low incomes). That it does so in fairly basic standards of housing is not in dispute, but that this is a substantial achievement should not go unrecognized.

If the market can and does fulfil housing needs, then all well and good. If it fails to do so then there is a responsibility for government to intervene. It is not necessary to argue that

Table 7.1 Household Income and Rents for Public and Private Rented Housing

		1994 (Jan–June)	1993	1992
Median Monthly Household Income	HK$			
Public Rental Housing		14,000	13,000	11,000
Permanent Private Housing		11,000	10,500	9,000
		16,500	15,300	13,500
Median Monthly Household Rent	HK$			
Public Rental Housing		1,006	950	871
Permanent Private Housing		950	899	811
		2,200	2,500	1,817
Median Rent-Income Ratio	%			
Public Rental Housing		9.9	9.4	9.4
Permanent Private Housing		8.0	7.9	8.2
		22.0	22.5	19.7

Source: Hong Kong Housing Authority.

there is intrinsic merit in housing provision by the state, but neither is it reasonable to argue for a massive withdrawal of the public sector when the market has consistently failed to meet the reasonable expectations of low income households. The existence of a 150,000 household waiting list for public rental housing provides compelling evidence of unsatisfied demand for basic, affordable housing.

The Failure of Privatization

Proponents of a smaller, even residual, role for public housing argue for privatization through the sale of flats to sitting tenants. However, in spite of the impressive economic performance of the Territory over the last ten years, there are many households nowhere near able to afford home ownership at anything other than give-away prices. The Sale of Flats to Sitting Tenants Scheme, launched in 1991, represented the Housing Authority's first attempt at privatization. It was a signal failure with only 7.5 per cent of tenants offered the chance opting to buy, despite a deep discount of 45 per cent of market prices. The reasons for this failure range from the standard of the dwellings offered for sale, the price relative to the low level of rent charged for the same dwellings, and the restrictive nature of the discount clawback in the event of resales within the first ten years after transfer.

Wong and Staley have argued for bolder privatization to be applied, in particular without restrictions on resale or clawback of the price discount at the time of purchase. This would undoubtedly enhance the attractiveness of this privatization scheme but at what price? The first buyers at such a deep discount must benefit, but even with substantial sales, problems of poor quality construction and maintenance will remain, problems compounded by the practical difficulties of managing multi-tenure blocks. The sales receipts generated would swell the Housing Authority's coffers, but the Authority is already cash-rich from its home ownership and commercial property operations, and from the renegotiation of its financial relationship with government in May 1994. Further, while the Authority is cash-rich, it is facing the most common development problem in Hong Kong today, namely a shortage of land for its identified construction programmes.

The net effect would be to transfer dwellings (and housing opportunities) out of the public sector and cash into the Authority's coffers, but without creating any compensating housing opportunities for lower-income groups.

Instead of seeking to minimize the role of public housing, there should be a recognition that public housing plays a significant role in the economic development of the Territory by providing subsidized housing to those who would otherwise be unable to afford adequate housing in the private market and hence providing a pool of labour prepared to work for lower wages, and at the same time reducing the social and political conflict arising out of poor or expensive housing conditions.

A transition of the Territory's economy from its manufacturing past to a services-led future is substantially underway with the large scale loss of manual jobs to China and other South and South-East Asian locations. This will only add to the pressures facing low-income households. As in the past, the provision of a supply of cheap housing will be a significant element of ensuring social and economic stability. Eroding that supply through privatization or higher rents will reverse the benefits that have been accumulated. Public housing needs to be constructed at a faster rate in order to meet these challenges, and in particular to meet the pressing needs of those trapped in poor housing conditions in the private rented sector, in squatter areas, or in temporary housing areas, seeking their turn through the waiting list.

Rather than seeking to dismantle the public housing sector the emphasis should be placed firmly on ensuring that the quantity and quality of public housing is a reasonable reflection of the state of economic and social development that has now been achieved. A prosperous society should seek to ensure a fair distribution of the results of that prosperity, and this could appropriately take the form of constructing new housing and upgrading the quality of the existing stock. Such a view appears to be shared by the Housing Authority who have significantly enhanced their programmes of construction, and upgrading of older estates. For the vast majority of the 46 per cent of the population living in publicly provided or supported rental housing this is the main priority. The government's commitments to rehouse all urban-area squatter settlements and temporary housing areas, together with the longer-term impact of increased immigration from China (both before and after 1997), all serve to compound the need for additional housing. The agenda for housing cannot become dominated by the push for home ownership.

An Alternative to Privatization

Instead of seeking to transfer dwellings out of the public sector, it is more appropriate to improve the physical standards of housing available, and the standards of management and maintenance offered by the Authority. This would respond far more directly to the concerns and aspirations of the vast majority of tenants. Housing is one of the most political of social welfare services in Hong Kong. Any shortcomings in standards of service are readily exposed to the full glare of publicity. This has been much in evidence since mid-1993 when the previous chairman of the Housing Authority, Sir David Akers-Jones resigned, in part, in response to a series of lively protests and demonstrations outside the Authority's headquarters.

Tenants protested about a number of key policies, particularly those involving rent increases and charging double rent to longer-standing tenants of improved financial means. Others made high-profile protests to draw attention to their campaigns for improvements to living conditions on their estates. The complaints voiced were many and varied but primarily related to the standards of day-to-day management, maintenance, security, and safety on housing estates. There were also objections to the Authority's lack of openness in taking major decisions on policies affecting tenants' daily lives, such as estate redevelopment or rent levels. Legislators publicly echoed these concerns in the newly politicized environment that followed the first direct elections to the Legislative Council.

The Housing Authority's response to this change in their operating environment has been to seek improved quality of service through a variety of quality-oriented programmes. This was first evident in the publication of the Housing Authority's Performance Pledges in July 1993, including eight related to estate management. These could be characterized as predominantly administrative in nature, (concerned with the Housing Department's processing of applications for various services, or inspection of deficiencies), and generally fell short of community expectations. However, it is important not to overlook the significance of the changes in attitude to tenants that was implicit in such pledges. One of the priorities was to improve the openness and responsiveness of the Authority and to raise the level of public esteem enjoyed by public housing. The causes of these concerns were clear, as identified in the 1993 policy address by Governor Patten who asked the Authority for '. . . improved commitments to prompt repairs and higher standards of maintenance; improved security measures on estates; and a long-term commitment to higher quality housing management'.

The maintenance function has been expanded with substantially increased budgets. In addition to providing additional resources, it was necessary to review management structures for planning and controlling the expenditure. Management responsibility for maintenance had traditionally been split between separate estate management and maintenance divisions, with control over the major expenditure being located within the maintenance division. One consequence of this line of management was that day-to-day repairs were being accorded lower priority. Contractors were naturally prioritizing those which were major in terms of value and works required. The result was delays and poor performance in day-to-day repairs, which were exactly the problems giving most cause for concern among tenants.

In response to this problem, and the availability of additional resources, a Minor Maintenance Section (MMS) has been set up to take charge of minor maintenance, and will be the primary point of contact for tenants with repair orders and queries. The intention is to empower estate management staff to discharge their 'client' functions on behalf of tenants more effectively, ensuring that day-to-day maintenance matters are accorded sufficient priority, and carried out to appropriate standards.

The re-engineering of the maintenance function however needs to go significantly deeper, particularly in empowering housing management. In this respect, user-friendly information technology is necessary so that an unresponsive service under the control of the maintenance division does not become an unwieldy system under the control of estate management. The Housing Department is currently developing a computerized solution to the management of day-to-day repairs.

In response to the call for higher standards of security on housing estates, a number of measures are being implemented. Security has been an issue of concern because of rising crime in a number of areas, although the reported crime rate associated with public housing is lower than that prevailing generally (approximately 52 cases per 10,000 population compared to approximately 140 cases per 10,000 population for the territory as a whole, according to Authority and police data). Nevertheless, the existence of concerns led to a decision to align standards of security for all housing blocks based on the prevailing standards for home ownership blocks. Tenants' feedback has been positive following a pilot scheme carried out in two buildings in the summer of 1994. These measures are similar to those developed in high-crime areas in other urban societies, and seem wholly appropriate in responding to tenant concerns.

The third issue identified in the 1993 policy address was the need to improve the quality of housing management. In response, the Housing Authority has sought to upgrade training of estate management staff and has improved its systems for communication. Also the Authority has reviewed existing channels of communication with tenants and announced, in November 1994, the creation of Estate Management Advisory Committees, including a degree of tenant participation.

Overall then there have been a number of significant financial and administrative improvements to the management and maintenance of public housing over the last two years, reflecting a broader change in attitudes to the public within public services, and the translation of this into a recognition of tenants as customers with all of the rights and respect that should naturally flow to customers. Although there is still a long way to go, this is clearly a welcome development.

Promoting Home Ownership

One of the most important factors in the expansion of demand for housing in Hong Kong is the strong and positive sentiment towards home ownership in Chinese societies. Ownership of the dwelling a household occupies is associated in popular culture with greater freedom and better economic returns. High rates of economic growth experienced since the mid-1980s have also acted as a catalyst to the emergence of a new middle class, and a resultant increase in demand for dwellings for owner occupation. The importance of the middle classes, both economically and politically, requires that these demands be taken seriously and hence the complexion of housing policy has undergone significant change from a purely residualist mode of rental housing for the lowest income households to one incorporating policies which promote and support home ownership.

There is no escaping the government's determination to increase the home ownership rate significantly and correspondingly reduce the scope of the government establishment involved in the provision and management of housing. Envious glances are cast towards Singapore with a home ownership rate greater than 80 per cent, largely in dwellings provided by the Housing Development Board.

The result is increasing emphasis on this tenure within the Long-term Housing Strategy (LTHS), the Territory's housing policy masterplan. This is evident in the home ownership rate in Hong Kong which is approximately 48 per cent, of which the public sector component amounts to about 10 per cent. The Housing Authority estimates that by 1997 home ownership in the Territory will reach 51 per cent with the public sector contributing 13 per cent.

The emphasis on home ownership was reaffirmed in the Housing Authority's mid-term review of the LTHS completed in 1994, and was reiterated in the broader review of housing policies announced by Dominic Wong Shing-wah on taking up the recreated post of housing secretary in February 1995.

Over the last five years, however, Hong Kong's residential sector has experienced marked inflation, peaking in the first quarter of 1994 prior to the announcement of government action to regulate prices, and a subsequent price fall. The roots of the inflation lie in a deep imbalance between supply and demand, and a number of distinctive features of the development and financing of the residential sector. The land supply restrictions have earlier been noted. Together with the extreme 'commodification' of housing (i.e. a situation where homes are 'assets', rather than locations of family life) this has resulted in high levels of speculative purchase and hoarding. The inevitable effect has been to exacerbate a pre-existing imbalance between the supply and demand for dwellings for owner occupation.

Price inflation has marginalized a sizeable group of new middle-class households, effectively barring them from home ownership. When allied to the income barrier to subsidized public housing this has led to the emergence over the last five years of an increasingly vocal group known as the 'sandwich class' trapped between these two predominant tenure sectors. The sandwich class as a group are very much a phenomenon of a strongly performing economy leading to significant growth in personal incomes, and a desire both for economic and also traditional reasons to invest savings in the residential property market. Despite their comparatively high levels of income, the government has made commitments to supporting the housing needs of the sandwich class through a specially designed and administered programme of loans and direct construction for subsidized sale, the Sandwich Class Housing Scheme, involving the construction of 10,000 flats by 1997, and the Sandwich Class Housing Loans Scheme, providing loans of up to 20 per cent of the purchase price to up to 13,000 eligible households.

This support however comes at a high price. Successive stages of the Sandwich Class Housing Loans Scheme have enjoyed increasingly generous financial support. The fourth and final stage offers applicants a deferred repayment loan of up to HK$600,000 at nominal interest rates. The Housing Authority has also followed suit in the provision of loans up to the same amount to entice longer-term and better-off public rental tenants to surrender their flats. The present value of such concessionary terms is approximately HK$308,900, an amount greater than the cost of construction of a new flat. Even taking into account the land cost element, the wisdom and equity of such generous loans seems questionable. Political expediency seems to have played a very strong part in determining this policy.

Stresses in Hong Kong's Housing Market

Whatever the government's direct role in supporting home ownership, there are compelling reasons to hope that the market will bear the main burden of allocating private housing. There are however a number of factors which make the housing markets of Hong Kong distinctive, and which affect their efficient functioning. There is then a further role for government in managing the markets for housing.

On the supply side, the shortage of developable land is undoubtedly the major factor that anyone seeking to ensure an efficient market would need to address. This problem has been compounded by an artificially low ceiling on the amount of land that may be consumed for residential development. Land in Hong Kong is owned by, or held on lease from, the government. Fearing an asset-stripping disposal of this most valuable of commodities in advance of its resumption of sovereignty, the Chinese side at the negotiations leading to the 1983 Joint Declaration successfully argued for a specific limit on land disposals to be overseen by the Sino-British Joint Land Commission. The imposition of a limit of 50 hectares per year, equivalent to the then prevailing levels of land disposal, has proven to be far too conservative and a major hindrance to effective market operation. Notwithstanding a more relaxed approach to these limits within the Commission over the last two years, the net effect has been a strangulation of land supply.

In addition to the rapid economic growth detailed earlier, one of the most significant short-term forces influencing the level of demand for housing, i.e. demographic changes, is being experienced. According to government statistics, the population of Hong Kong has increased by over 375,000 in the period 1989 to 1994. Current population and household projections have been revised upwards by 4,000–6,000 households per year or an additional 36,000–39,000 households per year between 1994 and 2000. The translation of this population increase into the demand for housing is a function of many factors, including incomes, costs, interest rates, opportunities, and corresponding risks, all of which are variable over time.

In addition, there is a significant number of the population within the 25–40 age group, the group most likely to be forming new households and setting up home independently. The age profile is also significant in that it is the 25–40 age group that is most likely to take on a mortgage for economic as well as family formation reasons.

The property markets in Hong Kong are also heavily influenced by 'confidence' — the future of the Territory, relations with China, and the performance of the economy all act as major determinants of market sentiment. The impending transfer of sovereignty and consequent changes in migration patterns inevitably impacts upon the propensity to purchase for occupation. Purchases for investment may be less affected, if there is confidence in the stability of the markets and the ability to liquidate and transfer investments should the need arise. For others Hong Kong is, and will continue to be, home and for many middle-class households where the need for a dwelling is best met in the home-purchase market. These two types of purchaser respond to different stimuli and yet they are com-peting in the same marketplace.

The substantial commodification which has occurred clearly poses fundamental questions of whether Hong Kong's housing markets are now geared too heavily towards the interests of investors and speculators rather than the needs of households seeking affordable accommodation, and whether additional steps are required, such as through the taxation system, to discourage such speculation until such time as the market is able to satisfy the needs of end users. Such overt manipulation of the housing markets, however rational, will be strongly resisted from many quarters as an interference in the natural functioning of the markets and may be seen as exceeding the bounds of government responsibilities in housing. The dilemma facing the government is clear, but the tendency to non-interventionism has generally prevailed.

The Government's Response to Affordability Problems

In response to these supply and affordability problems, Governor Patten announced, in March 1994, a 'Task Force on Land Supply and Property Prices' to investigate and make recommendations on the causes and size of the problem; the scope and means for providing more sites for public and private housing; the means of removing constraints on the development of sites caused by the lack of infrastructure; measures to speed up redevelopment; measures to discourage speculation; and ways of assisting the Housing Society and the Land Development Corporation to expand and speed up their redevelopment programmes. The announcement of the Task Force immediately took much of the heat out of the property market, dampening both prices and speculation, as an apprehensive public waited for signals as to how the market was to be corrected. The market has since shown a number of signs of limited upturn.

In the event, the Task Force took a '. . . cautious and incremental approach [in which] . . . market intervention is kept to the minimum necessary to remove distortion, ensure fair competition and protect the interests of genuine home buyers'. The Task Force identified four areas for attention in terms of returning the market to a healthy state and achieving affordability, namely: increasing the supply from both the public sector and the private sector; increasing the supply of land for development; streamlining the planning and development process; and limiting speculation in completed (and pre-completion) dwellings.

In addressing this supply deficiency, the Task Force put forward plans for an additional 45,000 and, if necessary 60,000 dwellings up to the end of the governments long-term housing strategy in 2001. This additional 45,000 dwellings production will comprise 20,000 publicly provided dwellings (including publicly provided home-ownership dwellings), 10,000 'Sandwich Class Housing Scheme' flats, and 15,000 private domestic flats, and will be met by accelerating the throughput of projects in the pipeline, increasing the density of development, and 'entrusting' developers to undertake necessary infrastructure works themselves. These are all welcome measures.

In order to facilitate the production of the public sector component, the Housing Authority's financial arrangements with the government were revised to allow more freedom and a Development Fund and HK$7 billion in loans, were provided to allow the Housing Society to advance the Sandwich Class Housing Scheme. Finally, the Task Force indicated that 'building covenants would be introduced for redevelopment schemes to increase the certainty of the building completion date'. The creation of improved financial arrangements with the Authority and the Society are clearly appropriate steps in seeking to boost supply.

The government has identified 120 hectares of land for

residential development of which 70 hectares was earmarked for the 45,000 dwellings programme expansion. The remaining 50 hectares are to be held in reserve. These steps are again appropriate and respond directly to the needs identified, although it is premature at this stage to comment on their efficacy.

The Planning and Development Department was asked to assume overall responsibility for assessing the scale and composition of demand for both public and private housing, and also for undertaking a comprehensive assessment of redevelopment potential throughout the Territory. These are projects of long-term significance in that they seek to ensure the effective planning for changing needs rather than the reaction to current needs which has preoccupied and dominated much of housing policy in the Territory for the last forty years.

The most contentious element of the programme put forward by the Task Force was the attempt to limit and discourage speculation. The scale of speculation is revealed in the fact that 10 per cent of the sales of residential units between February 1992 and March 1994 involved short-term resales, and 43 per cent involved properties first offered for sale after 31 January 1992. This signifies that there was very active trading in new properties, and that the needs of end users were often treated secondary to those of speculators. In particular it was believed that many of the new dwellings being traded were originally sold by internal sale to persons connected with property companies.

A second effect of speculation is to keep completed units vacant. The Task Force carried out a sample survey of 10,078 dwellings (i.e. 31.7 per cent) in large developments completed in 1992. It revealed that 17.9 per cent were still vacant at the end of April 1994. A further sample survey of 17,544 dwellings (i.e. 69.9 per cent) in large developments completed in 1993 revealed that 40.5 per cent were still vacant at the end of April 1994. Nearly half of the units completed in 1993 and held vacant were held by developers or by individuals who had purchased blocks of flats in the same development, suggesting internal sales. Further analysis showed that 'a relatively higher percentage of the flats sold through private sales remained vacant for a longer period of time, as compared to those sold openly to the public'.

Hoarding of flats and keeping them vacant as a means of

retaining flexibility (and driving up the price through artificial shortages) may be a rational act on the part of an individual investor, but housing is such an important item of consumption that such actions should be heavily discouraged, either by punitive taxation (on profits or through the rating system) or by (less radical) administrative controls that discourage such speculative purchase.

The government, not surprisingly, took the latter option, including: limiting the number of internal sales to no more than 10 per cent of all sales; limiting forward sales to not earlier than nine months prior to the issue of a Certificate of Compliance or Consent to Assign (i.e. prior to the building being ready for occupation); and prohibiting resales prior to the issue of a Certificate of Compliance or Consent to Assign. Further, the initial deposit was raised to 10 per cent of the purchase price, with an automatic forfeiture of 5 per cent if the purchaser fails to complete, or assigns the benefit of the sale to a third party.

The full impact of improving housing and land supply and changes in the planning and development processes will only be realized in the medium to long term. The impact of the attempts to control speculation were seen immediately. Prices quickly dropped back 10–15 per cent, and market sentiment turned decidedly cooler. Transactions at the end of 1994 were down both in volume (to approximately half of the 13,000 sale and purchase agreements per month in March), and in price.

In other respects, the measures are unduly timid. They do not introduce taxation of capital gains or any penalty rating of empty properties. These remedies have been applied in many other countries. They effectively reduce hoarding and hence release vacant units on to the market reducing prices in one move.

Three key questions emerge from this analysis of housing in Hong Kong's current economic and social transformation. Firstly, do housing standards and the broader housing environment enjoyed by the mass of the population meet reasonable expectations? If not, what steps can those responsible for the design and implementation of housing policy take to ensure that housing standards properly reflect the new found prosperity of Hong Kong as a whole, and that good quality housing is not confined to high achievers in economic terms?

Secondly, how can housing markets be managed to ensure that the needs of end users are met by good quality, affordable housing, while at the same time allowing prices to govern supply and demand? This is likely to remain one of the key issues in determining housing policy over the short to medium term, and possibly even longer. It is likely to be resolved only when land supply is substantially improved.

The third question is that of determining and achieving an appropriate tenure balance. Home ownership remains popular and is likely to continue to enjoy a privileged position in housing policy. However, what happens to those not able to afford home ownership, or simply preferring to rent? What standards of housing should be provided? Should public rented housing be seen as a poor-quality, second-best option, or does the public rented sector have a viable future as a high-quality service?

In respect of the first question, it can be stated confidently that the standards of public housing are in need of continuous improvement, and that the standards of the older public housing still in use are now woefully short of those appropriate for the 1990s, let alone the start of the twenty-first century. Housing continues to consume approximately 10 per cent of public expenditure. This must be maintained, if not enlarged to meet the legitimate and reasonable aspirations of ordinary citizens. The standards of newly designed public housing are appropriate given the realities of space and financial restrictions. However, the standards of older public housing must be improved by extensive, accelerated renovation programmes, and by the improvement of maintenance and security programmes as previously described.

The apparent conflict between free market forces and the need to ensure that housing markets work in the interests of all sections of society is both conceptually and practically the most difficult. Left to their own devices markets can degenerate into vehicles of exploitation in times of shortage. In the longer term, the release of substantial additional land is the most important contribution that any government can make to the efficient functioning of the local housing markets to meet genuine end user demand for housing. Failing such steps being taken before July 1997, the new administration will be well advised to implement a change of policy immediately on resumption of power so as to restore a natural longer-term equilibrium to the operation of the market. In the short term however, a continued programme of demand management and steps to control market manipulation by sectors of the real estate industry are both necessary and unavoidable.

The third question concerns the most appropriate tenure balance and the future of public rental housing. Clearly tenure preferences are a matter for the individual (in the absence of taxation-based distortions). It is appropriate for government policy to work to meet these preferences as far as possible. The convergence of values between government and a majority of citizens is thus a common starting point for longer-term housing policy, supporting the further expansion of home ownership. Nevertheless, in the face of a high-priced, home-ownership sector, it will take a long time to realize this ambition. In the meantime, housing policies must be supportive of all tenures. In this respect the evidence suggests that serious attempts are being made to improve the standards of public housing in response to higher expectations, and an awareness of the need to improve effectiveness in the use of scarce resources. There is, however, a sizeable legacy of older housing in both the public and the private sector that constitutes a valid area of concern for society and which must be improved in recognition of the material economic and social advances of Hong Kong society as a whole.

The significance of housing, politically, economically, and socially, demands a coherent approach integrating public- and private-sector initiatives. There is considerable evidence that this is now the preferred way forward. Although the years of 'positive non-interventionism' have left us with a legacy of chronically over-priced and hence unaffordable housing in the private sector, government has gradually increased its intervention in the face of mounting problems arising from the over-commodification of housing and inefficiencies (from a users perspective) in the housing market. This has culminated in overt regulation over the last 18 months; from this it will be difficult to retreat. In the longer term, a return to purer market economics may be appropriate, but in the short term the shortages of land and the delays inherent in the construction process render such non-interventionist approaches over-optimistic and misguided.

8. The Environment and the Political Economy of Hong Kong

William Barron

Hong Kong's rapid economic transformation has led to a widening gap between its income and the environmental quality normally commensurate with such wealth. While incomes have risen steadily, the overall quality of the air, water, and land has declined, in some cases beyond the nuisance stage to the point where there are evident consequences for public health. It is likely that overall environmental quality will continue to decline, despite an increasing ability to pay for a safer, cleaner, and more pleasing environment and a growing awareness of its importance. While the loss of unpriced environmental services in the face of rising money income is unfortunately not uncommon around the world, Hong Kong's present development–environment trade-off represents a very poor bargain.

This chapter argues that despite commendable (though often belated) initiatives to address pressing environmental problems, it is the current Hong Kong government's own agenda (particularly its massive reclamation works and the economic consequences stemming from them) that is likely to preclude substantial overall environmental improvement. This predicament in which the government's own agenda works counter to its professed concern for the environment, and indeed its own actions for environmental protection, stems from the absence of an effective mechanism by which the particular interests of government's economic planners may be objectively weighed against broader concerns.

The key role played by the government's own agenda is also reflected in the way other criteria enter into decisions about the acceptability of proposed environmental measures (e.g. postponing the switch from diesel to petrol in 1990, because it might have added to general price inflation), and in the preference for direct controls (e.g. outright bans on some type of activity) rather than economic instruments (e.g. incentives for polluters to move in the desired direction). While this preference for rather blunt environmental policy instruments is sometimes justified when compliance-monitoring costs are considered, the basic motive here appears to be to minimize administrative costs to governmental regulatory agencies, regardless of the economic inefficiencies imposed on the polluters as a result.

Because government policy and the government's infrastructure plans are of such importance in the future of Hong Kong's environment, the transition of sovereignty in 1997 is of special interest. While it is unlikely that 1997 will bring any rapid shift in the government's stance to environmental issues, it will be an opportunity to re-evaluate plans for new infrastructure, plans that are closely identified with the outgoing British administration.

Indications of Environmental Quality

In general, Hong Kong enjoys better environmental quality than most of its neighbours, with the notable exception of Singapore. However, Hong Kong is the richest economy in the region (and indeed one of the richest in the world). Being cleaner than Shanghai or Bangkok is not really the point. In fact, Hong Kong's air and water quality do not meet Hong Kong's own internationally accepted quality standards in many respects. Moreover, things are likely to get worse before they get better.

While the health effects of poor air quality are often subtle and long term, there are already clear indications of effects on people's health leading to growing concerns about the full extent of damage resulting from the present and projected future levels of air pollution. Much of the Territory's marine environment is severely degraded and likely to get worse. Swimming is inadvisable at many local beaches, while pollution has forced relocation of fish farms and raised concerns about the safety of seafood. Adding to the ecological stresses from inadequately treated sewage and industrial effluent are concerns over the long-term effects of the massive reclamation and urban redevelopment. On land, much of the rural area has been despoiled by haphazard conversion to cargo container storage sites. Many of the New Territories' remaining natural ecosystems in areas outside (and in some cases adjacent to or even within) the country parks are being lost to development as Hong Kong's 'rural areas' turn 'suburban'.

The Development–Environment Nexus in Hong Kong

Hong Kong, which has moved rapidly from a low-income, labour-intensive economy, to a service-driven and high-income economy, finds itself with a legacy of environmental degradation out of balance with its needs and ability to pay. With a few notable exceptions, such as the extensive country park system, until about the mid-1980s the government — and arguably the people of Hong Kong — generally placed relatively little value on environmental amenities and services. This was particularly true at the margin, i.e. in the specific trade-offs between attaining the *next* increment of low-cost output and accepting a further small decline in the quality of the air, water, or land resources.

In the terminology of economists, the government — with the apparent acquiescence of the general population — permitted most environmental impacts to be treated as 'external costs', costs that legally (and often with minimal social criticism) could be ignored by those responsible for creating them. Hence, when an industrialist, farmer, land developer, or service provider (e.g. bus owner) assessed the benefits and costs to himself (i.e. his 'private costs') of such things as the type of fuel or equipment to use, or how to dispose of wastes, this assessment typically excluded the consequences to the natural environment and to human health and safety. Again, using the terminology of economists, environmental 'property rights' lay largely with those wishing to use the air, water, and land to dispose of unwanted waste products, rather than with those who suffered as a consequence.

Given the economic and environmental situation in Hong Kong up to the mid-1980s, this highly skewed split in the assignment of environmental property rights was not necessarily inappropriate. Such an argument rests on two related considerations. First, with the lower incomes in Hong Kong at the time, people may well have preferred to give up a rather large amount of environmental quality in return for an opportunity to share in the increased short-term gain associated with low *financial* costs of production. The second point is that with a relatively healthy state of the environment at the time (i.e. one could still swim in Victoria Harbour, the New Territories were still largely undeveloped, and air quality outside of industrial areas was generally good) the absorptive capacity of the air, water, and land was still sufficient to accommodate additional wastes without long-term damage to the underlying ability of these media to provide essential services to everyone (i.e. plentiful and safe seafood, uncontaminated soil, and unpoisoned air).

This said, it is important to point out that even when incomes were low and the environment was relatively clean, market signals did not operate to check socially harmful environmental impacts. As a result, many opportunities for efficient improvements in the management of the environment as economic development proceeded were missed.

Trade-offs at the Margin

When faced with such a trade-off under conditions where one enjoys a relatively high level of environmental quality and a relatively low level of money income, it is reasonable that the value placed on each additional increment of money income is rather high and concurrently that the value placed on incremental losses of environmental quality is relatively low. Giving up a unit of something which at the margin has a relatively low value for a unit of something with a high value at the margin is a rational and indeed prudent decision. Yet, the obvious corollary is that when incomes become relatively high and environmental quality low, it is likewise rational and prudent to value the trade-off of a bit more money income versus further environmental deterioration quite differently. And indeed, this reassessment of the terms of an acceptable economy–environment trade-off has taken place in Hong Kong over the past decade.

Valuing Unpriced Goods and Services

The appropriate trade-off between environmental quality and other goals is relatively simple to identify in concept. In practice however, the matter is rarely so simple. Typically, much of the benefit of environmental improvement is not readily measurable in money terms and hence the value people place on it is difficult to precisely determine. When all values are measured in a common unit (e.g. dollars), trade-off assessments may be quite objective and precise. Trade-offs involving comparisons of values not measured in a common unit are inherently more subjective and inexact.

Historically, many of the most important types of environmental problems have not been amenable to direct negotiations between the polluters and those most directly affected. Hence the 'free market' solution to balancing the interests of various parties made familiar by economist Ronald Coase is often impractical. In response to such problems, environmental decision-making generally involves government doing what the market tends not to do well — appropriately valuing the importance of the largely non-monetized environmental values against the monetary and other costs of actions for environmental protection.

Such assessments involve weighing of monetized values against non-monetized ones, and addressing the question of how to distribute the cost burden. 'Making the polluter pay' is a principle espoused by the Hong Kong government, but in practice, even when the principle is adhered to, it is typically applied only to pollution above a level the government has determined to be permissible.

The Government and the Environmental Valuation Process

The Hong Kong government has taken important steps in changing the balance between the rights of specific private groups (e.g. farmers, industrialists, vehicle owners) to dispose of the waste products of their activities, or to alter land and seascapes as inexpensively as possible, relative to the rights of people living or working nearby and of the general population to an acceptably safe environment. What had been accepted behaviour from polluters is now often subject to severe restriction because, in the 'judgement' of the responsible government agencies, damage to the well-being of the population and to the natural ecology from uncontrolled pollution of specific types should be valued more highly than the costs imposed on the polluters to lessen such damage. In such assessments, governmental agencies in Hong Kong have generally attempted to act as the impartial arbitrator when setting standards, balancing as objectively as possible the interests of particular groups against the general interest.

Assessing Environmental Values

Growing awareness of the importance of the environment in Hong Kong, particularly among the better educated and more widely travelled, parallels such development elsewhere in the world. Though coming somewhat later than in the older industrialized economies, environmental awareness and calls for action from Hong Kong's non-governmental organizations (NGOs), were often stronger and earlier than similar calls from NGOs in neighbouring economies. With that noted, it is important to point out that, in the 1980s, it was the *government* which took the lead in promoting awareness of the importance of environmental services. The government also provided the lead in the gradual re-assignment of environmental property rights, stressing the rights of people to be protected from the effects of severe environmental degradation. From the start of environmental action in Hong Kong, the government typically saw itself in the role of leader. This view has crucial implications for today's environmental decision-making in Hong Kong.

The Government as the Environmental Leader

In the 1980s the government probably believed it was leading a largely indifferent, even reluctant, population in setting more appropriate terms for trade-offs between the pace of economic expansion and level of environmental quality. Indeed, the government still seems to believe that it remains in front of public opinion on the environment.

As noted above, in concept, the appropriate (i.e. the most efficient) level of environmental protection is where the marginal benefits of the next increment in protection equal the marginal cost of taking that step. In Hong Kong's governmental system, the executive branch of government itself makes this assessment. In some cases, this has resulted in the government taking strong action despite limited community pressure and in face of the strident opposition of those who bear most of the costs. For example, the government banned, as of June 1988, the keeping of livestock in urban areas despite protests from farmers. Against strong opposition from affected industries and more broadly based concerns from the business community, it banned the use of high-sulphur fuel oil in 1990. In the face of continuing concerns about its impact on the ongoing movement of industrial jobs to Guangdoung, the government has proceeded with its step-by-step imposition of water quality control zones setting strict requirements on effluent discharges.

Yet despite these commendable (and ultimately widely accepted) actions, in a number of other cases government has dealt with problems hesitantly or not at all. For example, transport-related air pollution remains a major concern and is likely to get much worse before it gets better. While the plan for the diesel-to-petrol switch for light commercial vehicles which was shelved in 1990 due to perceived conflicts with the government's inflation-fighting agenda was revived in 1995, only in September 1995 did the government put forward a specific proposal. At the time of writing, this proposal is before the Legislative Council.

With regard to sewage treatment, despite strong opposition by environmental groups and marine scientists to the government's plan for minimal treatment prior to discharge through a long marine outfall, it was only after the national government of China refused to accept this plan that the Hong Kong government reconsidered alternative levels and types of treatment.

While many in Hong Kong argue that waste incineration (especially with co-generation of electricity) is worth careful further consideration, the government continues to insist that landfills *alone* should be the final disposal option.

In each of these cases and others which might be cited, the government decided upon a specific course of action after limited consultation — and arguably little true dialogue — with the population at large, or with those most affected. The government itself typically decides upon the scope of studies to identify policy options and solicits public input *after* the consultants have made their report. This may result in option assessments in which important factors are left out of the scope of the study, since no independent advice is sought at this stage. It also encourages decision-makers to select one, or a few, preferred policy positions and to then approach the public consultation exercise as an opportunity to explain and defend a particular choice rather than as a time to engage in a truly open discussion with concerned groups about a variety of options which still might be seriously considered.

Leader or Sole Judge?

Because it is recognized that assessments of benefits and costs by particular segments of society may be at odds with the benefits and costs as felt by society as a whole, businesses and individual citizens are no longer given this freedom in Hong Kong, nor in most of the world. Rather, some ostensibly unbiased entity is given the authority to weigh the total social benefits against the total social costs when deciding whether actions that damage the environment are to be allowed, and if so, to what extent. The question then is whether a government agency is likely to be unbiased in valuing the environmental consequences of its own preferred programmes. At least within the Environmental Protection Department (EPD) and some other parts of government, environmental quality is viewed as very important. This is reflected in decisions taken over the past several years to severely restrict, or ban, previously common actions on the part of industrialists, farmers, and private motorists, as well as in efforts to implement the polluter pays principle even for publicly provided services such as waste water treatment. Yet, environmental advocates in Hong Kong are increasingly concerned that the government is now tending to give a low *implicit* value to the environment relative to other goals when it comes to its own agenda.

Data Gaps and Selected Targeting

Before exploring in greater detail the interplay between the government's own agenda and the environment, it is useful to consider the matter of the gaps in our knowledge of the environment in Hong Kong and the environmental consequences of specific actions. With an effective environmental monitoring system it is possible to track continuing changes in the ambient environment, and potentially, to correlate such changes with exogenous developments (e.g. rising economic output in specific industries) and with policy initiatives (e.g. a mandate to those industries to use cleaner fuel). Unfortunately, comprehensive monitoring systems are often difficult and expensive to develop and maintain, and they are rarely, if ever, as comprehensive as analysts would like.

EPD began annual publication of various environmental quality indicators in 1989. Although there have been some changes in the level of reporting and significant gaps continue to exist, the information published over the past six years provides important indications of vital aspects of environmental quality in Hong Kong and some insights into the actual or likely impact of various economic, social, and governmental policy developments.

For example, with a public record starting in 1988 on sulphur dioxide (SO_2) and particulate levels in Kwai Chung it was possible to document the high background levels of these pollutants in 1988 and 1989 and to show the dramatic drop (by 80 per cent) in SO_2 and the more moderate drop in particles following the ban in July 1990 on high sulphur fuel oil by industry. It happened that at the urging of the local district board an extensive respiratory health survey was conducted in 1989 for children in that area with a follow-up study in 1991 and 1992. These health surveys demonstrated that children in this industrial area of Hong Kong had an 'excess risk' of various upper respiratory symptoms and a greater frequency of visiting a doctor to treat these symptoms compared to children living in Hong Kong Island's Southern District where the air was much cleaner. The follow-up health survey in 1991 to 1992 showed that after the air quality improvements this excess risk was largely eliminated. At a minimum, the air quality improvement as a result of the ban on high sulphur fuel resulted in an immediate cost-saving to the local community in the form of reduced doctor consultations and related expenditures.

Such instances of a relatively well-documented environmental pollution problem and its response to a strong policy initiative are not all that common. While the roof-top air quality monitors provide an indication of chronic exposures (i.e. long-term background dosage), they typically are able to reveal little about acute exposure (i.e. short-term, very high dosage) whether to people in the case of air pollution. Likewise, present water-quality monitoring cannot give a comprehensive picture of the impact on marine organisms (some of which enter the human food chain) from marine water pollution.

In other words, we may say with some confidence that the people of Kwai Chung experienced much better air quality after June 1990 compared to at least the two previous years and that their children needed doctor consultations less often when the air improved. But we do not know what the longer-term effects are and we do not know the effects on these same children of their continuing exposure to short-term high concentrations of diesel vehicle smoke as they walk and play in their neighbourhoods.

Likewise, we may know that the ability of a certain marine area to support aquatic life has been greatly reduced in the near term by increased turbidity in the water due to dredging, but we do not know with much certainty what species might be severely threatened (or perhaps brought to extinction), what the long-term effects on the overall ecosystem will be and what amount of toxic material stirred up by the dredging is entering our food chain.

We are learning more about Hong Kong's environment, but present understanding is incomplete and often more suggestive than definitive. Hence, decisions about when and how to act typically depend on the views of decision-makers regarding (1) the possible (rather than known) nature and level of specific impacts; and (2) the likelihood (risk) of some consequence if they act or fail to act in a certain way. This provides room to manoeuvre for policy makers with a mixed agenda, since a particular action or the lack of it may be defended in terms of the *presumed* nature and level of *potential* environmental impacts and subjective assessments concerning the actual risk and the acceptability of it.

The Government's Agenda and the Environment

If asked how the environment fits in with the plans and goals of the Hong Kong government, a governmental spokesperson would likely say that environmental protection and improve-ment has a high priority and would point to a wide range of activities including development of improved sewage treat-ment systems, livestock waste control, creation of water quality control zones, industrial air and water emission stand-ards, fuel quality mandates, noise controls, etc. Yet, while the government is clearly active in promoting environmental protection in many specific ways, there are other items high on the government's agenda which tend to add to environ-mental stress and limit actions to address past damage. The most important of these items is physical infrastructure deve-lopment (especially reclamation) and the economic activity it is designed to support.

Infrastructure Development and the Environment

Concerns about infrastructure development are largely related to the Port and Airport Development Strategy (PADS) and the further reclamation works for the more easterly portion of Victoria Harbour (i.e. Eastern Kowloon). This programme is driven by a vision of Hong Kong's long-term economic role in the regional transshipment of goods and people.

In order for this vision to be realized, large parts of Victoria Harbour and adjacent areas are being filled in to increase the size of the core urban area, a new airport is to be built and serviced by road and rail transport, and vastly expanded port facilities are to be built.

The environmental degradation associated with these infra-structure projects occurs directly and immediately through marine dredging and filling on a scale that by any interna-tional comparison can only be described as 'massive'. It also occurs indirectly over the longer term through the conse-quences of expanded marine shipping, expansion of the core urban area (with reduced access to the environmental ser-vices provided by a large marine harbour), and much higher projected volumes of commercial road traffic.

PADS actually consists of two largely independent transport-infrastructure development efforts — the Airport Core Projects (ACP) and the Port Development Strategy (PDS). The ACP is composed of the new airport at Chek Lap Kok, the airport railway from Central, and road projects involving extensive tunnels and bridges and nearly 1,700 hectares of reclamation. The total cost is estimated by the government to be about HK$83 billion for the airport and HK$110 billion for the entire ACP effort.

The PDS will be implemented in four phases up to 2011. It involves four massive container terminals (numbers 10 through to 13) with additional terminals tentatively planned for the post-2011 period. Terminals 10 through to 13 are to be constructed on 460 hectares of reclamation off the north-eastern end of Lantau Island. PDS is designed to accommodate (or rather to encourage) a projected 186 per cent increase in cargo volume shipped through Hong Kong in 2011, compared with that in 1994. Most of the additional cargo handling is for transshipment overland to China. Even with a new rail cargo line, PDS will add greatly to road transport demands in the already congested Western New Territories. PDS is estimated to cost roughly HK$61 billion (in 1994 prices), with over one-third of the budget for government-funded reclamation and infrastructure to support the privately owned terminals. Government funding is expected to be offset eventually through premium payments and land sales.

Further reclamation works will reduce the area of the harbour by roughly another 400 hectares. These projects will, after the closing of the present airport at Kai Tak, fill in much of Kowloon Bay. At the same time, reclamation is to be extended along the middle and eastern portions of the north shore of Hong Kong Island, smoothing out the shoreline to the northerly limits of the ACP-related extensions into the harbour. The harbour would then take on the characteristics of a short, moderately wide river or a strait with relatively uniform shorelines in place of the present harbour's many bays and inlets. Most of the further reclamation works are still in the planning stage, but they form a consistent part of the Metroplan Selected Strategy.

The major environmental concerns raised by the ACP, the PDS, and the further reclamation works are similar — the effects on marine water quality due to the reclamation works themselves and the long-term environmental impact of the expanded core urban space and economic activities that the projects are designed to encourage. In reclaimed areas, it is often necessary to first remove old sediments, since these provide an unstable foundation for the new material. In areas near older industrial sites, particularly along Kowloon, the sediments requiring removal are highly contaminated by decades of uncontrolled industrial toxic effluent, including heavy metals. These can enter the food chain and affect human health as well as have other impacts on the local ecology. The removal and reburying of contaminated muds in 1994 involved some cases of illegal dumping and complaints from fishermen that the muds buried near their fishing grounds were resulting in reduced and contaminated fish catches.

Hong Kong's new land created through reclamation comes largely by drawing up sands from selected sites in the eastern waters of the Territory, carrying it by ship, and placing it along the southern shores of Kowloon, the northern shore of Hong Kong Island, and along the north-eastern shore of Lantau Island. The new airport will require about 76 million cubic metres of marine fill, while the PDS will require over 200 million. Assuming that the further reclamation works required proportionately the same volume of fill per hectare as the ACP, this will entail removal and dumping of another 18 million cubic metres. Imagine a cube of sand roughly 670 metres on a side — well over twice as high as Hong Kong's tallest building! In the process of drawing up the sand, transporting it and dumping it at the new location, some of the material is lost, causing some habitats to be buried and others to be affected by greatly increased suspended material in the water and a reduction in light penetration. While careful planning and care in operation can eliminate or reduce some impacts on the marine ecology, other impacts are unavoidable.

With regard to the PDS, environmental impacts stemming from transshipment of containers between Hong Kong's planned new marine terminals and China is a major concern. Traffic congestion and resulting effects on mobility and air pollution are already one of the territory's most pressing environmental problems, a problem projected to get much worse. The port development will increase container transshipment through Hong Kong several fold compared to present levels. Large container trucks are already a major source of pollution and road congestion in the western New Territories. While a new rail line and a new road link will eventually ease part of the added burden on the existing road system, traffic levels and the resulting pollution and congestion problems in the area must increase. Unfortunately, the environmental impact assessment (EIA) for the PDS did not consider such 'off-site' impacts.

The ACP will also add to traffic, but the new airport rail link should help to ease some existing road congestion in the Western Kowloon area. Overall, environmental concerns over ACP relate primarily to the impacts on the marine environment. In contrast, for the PDS marine environmental concerns are in some respects overshadowed by the off-site impacts of air pollution, noise, and congestion.

So far as the further reclamation works in the harbour are concerned, the additional issues include impacts on wind patterns which may alter pollution dispersion in the core urban area, the congestion impacts of adding population and associated transport and other facilities to the core urban area, as well as the visual impacts of fundamentally changing the balance of water, the built environment, and the mountains.

Assessing the Impact of the Infrastructure Programmes

Several points are important to stress with regard to how the environmental impacts of the government's own infrastructure projects were evaluated:

1. No EIA was carried out prior to the decision to proceed with the ACP, the PDS, or the further reclamation works.
2. Despite the obvious potential for major cumulative effects, no EIA has been carried out for the entire reclamation, nor for its major subdivisions (e.g. the ACP as a whole).
3. EIAs are (or will be) carried out on only the individual projects which comprise the ACP, the PDS, and further reclamation works as a means of identifying cost-effective mitigation measures to lessen the associated environmental damage *so far as this can be done within the already approved project design.*

Governor Patten's 1995 policy speech noted that the government would ensure 'that the environmental impacts of development projects are fully assessed at the planning stage'. This policy seems to be aimed at private development projects.

Their possible application to governmental ones is unclear. What is clear is that, given the very limited public input into the design of the ACP, the PDS, and the further reclamations, only the particular interests and concerns of the government planners who commissioned these design studies were certain to be reflected in what the studies looked at and how potential environmental impacts are assessed. It has been claimed, for example, that the terms of reference for the consultants hired to study the potential for further reclamation in Victoria Harbour was to determine the maximum extent to which the harbour could be filled in *without unduly obstructing shipping.*

At this point, the construction of the new airport at Chek Lap Kok is a fact. Remaining debates and concerns are focused on the details (e.g. how and where to construct the fuel storage depot, and how to enhance the survival potential of the Chinese white dolphin population). While the government and certain directly interested parties have argued strongly that the *full* port expansion is essential to Hong Kong's continued prosperity, this view does not seem to be particularly widely or strongly held by the citizenry at large, or even by much of the Hong Kong business community. This is not to say that most groups are actively opposed to the port expansion, but simply that serious questions seem to remain in the public's mind and that what support exists (beyond that from groups with a clear vested interest) is thin and mixed at best.

Also, while the decision about the airport at Chek Lap Kok was in many important respects largely an all-or-nothing undertaking, the proposed port expansion is segmented into distinct phases. Undertaking the initial phases is not contingent upon a decision to definitely undertake later phases.

It is important to stress that opposition to the port expansion is not opposition to Hong Kong playing an expanded role in the China trade. Opponents point out that much of the value to Hong Kong from this trade comes from the trade-related services for the movement of these goods and that such benefits could still be enjoyed, even if much of the growth in the physical transshipment of the cargo occurred in nearby new and upgraded mainland ports, so long as the territory remained the financial and management centre for the trade.

In the view of opponents, the added economic benefits of physically moving so much of the increased trade through Hong Kong would be far outweighed by the environmental costs of the terminal construction and cargo transport through Hong Kong to and from China.

It is the present government's accelerating activities to embed its own vision of Hong Kong's long-term economic future as the physical transshipment point for much of the China trade (rather than simply its financial and management centre) that has the local environmental community most concerned about the longer-term environmental 'quality of life' here.

Policy Instruments for Environmental Management

Surprisingly, given the Hong Kong government's continued vocal adherence to the principle of a *laissez-faire* approach to the economy, economic incentives have not been viewed with much favour in the environmental area (though they have in other areas such as managing road-transport demand). Various evaluation criteria influence the choice of the type of policy instrument to achieve a specific policy objective and different interest groups will naturally tend to highlight the criteria of most concern to themselves. For example, affected polluters may be most concerned about the complexity of compliance, while the larger business community focuses on whether compliance is likely to be obtained at the least possible cost. Environmental advocacy groups may prefer to see management approaches which minimize the potential for non-compliance. In this assessment it is important to recognize that the environmental regulatory agency responsible for the management has its own concerns and as a result may favour certain types of policy instruments over others. In Hong Kong, environmental management is typically through command and control (C&C). C&C measures, while often demonstrably less efficient in principle than economic incentives, have the advantages of being administratively easier to implement and more predictable in outcome than comparable economic incentives.

Bans are the simplest form of command and control. EPD has utilized bans wherever possible as a basic policy tool. The use of such bans (e.g. on livestock farming in urban areas, on the use of high-sulphur fuel oil, on the use of incineration in the longer-term solid waste strategy, and the proposed ban on new light-diesel vehicles) might be justifiable when all the factors are considered. However, the use of bans in Hong Kong's environmental policy to date almost certainly has much to do with EPD giving its own concerns priority over those of outside groups, whether these be the business community or environmental advocacy groups.

In some cases, despite its *laissez-faire* motto, the government appears to have valued ease of implementation and minimization of the potential for visible compliance failure sufficiently highly to opt to pay for much of the costs itself, rather than 'make the polluter pay'. In some cases, this has involved such a retreat from the principles of economic efficiency that there appears to be little incentive left, even when the polluter must pay in some fashion (e.g. the industrial waste water surcharge).

The Way Forward

Hong Kong will continue to have an 'executive-led government' in the post-1997 era, but this need not preclude wider participation in the process of assessing environment–development trade-offs. The executive should (1) become far more open and transparent in its assessment activities, and (2) begin to engage in a true consultative process at the earliest stage of option evaluation.

Perhaps most basic to attaining such changes is to have the terms of reference for preliminary policy-option reviews open to outside comment. If the initial study of options is consciously or inadvertently biased in one direction or another, then the findings and all subsequent plans are in question. It may be as simple as 'if you don't ask the right questions, you are unlikely to get the right answers', or at worst, a matter of 'garbage in, garbage out'. It is common in Hong Kong today for environmental advocacy groups, business organizations, and others to feel that they are excluded from the assessment process until after the government has firmed up its preferred position, and that the government position is the result of an inadequately designed study of possible policy options.

Two factors seem likely to force much greater attention on the process by which the environment is assessed. First, the reclamation works have now reached such a scale — even at only a fraction of their ultimate planned level — that they directly and visibly affect a large part of the population. This is no longer a matter of the average person having seen a few government publicity maps carefully drawn to show the beneficial aspects of the planned expansions in the land area. It is a matter of millions of people seeing for themselves the already greatly reduced harbour area as they walk near the harbour or wait for a ferry. The impact is far more dramatic for those many thousands of residents who venture up to Victoria Peak and other high vantage points with friends and family.

The second factor likely to raise awareness of how damaging it can be to allow a few civil servants impose their own personal preferences on the very landscape we all share is the likelihood of the Legislative Council (Legco) becoming a more active forum for environmental policy debates.

In its authority to authorize funds, Legco has a potentially powerful, if rather blunt, instrument. Legco cannot 'fine tune' government policy. It can only agree, or fail to agree, to fund specific programmes. If there is an active spirit of co-operation between the executive and Legco, legislative councillors can help to shape government policies, while the executive seeks to ensure that its programmes are acceptable, minimizing the possibility that funds will be blocked. If this spirit of co-operation fails to develop, it will be business as usual. The government can package its programmes to make it difficult for Legco to block them (e.g. presenting to Legco only the government's preferred programme and threatening to withdraw it without an alternative submission if funding is not approved).

It is beyond the scope of this chapter to predict the political structure that will emerge in the Special Administrative Region. It is, however, important not to allow the change to demobilize activism on behalf of the environment. While it seems likely that the 'business community' will have an important influence over policy in the new government, as it always has in the British administration, this does not mean that efficient trade-offs between economic development and environmental protection cannot continue to be made.

Indeed, one significant feature of business' involvement in Hong Kong's environmental affairs in recent years has been the active role of some businesses (in particular, large firms and those in technology- or service-oriented industries) in promoting greater action on the environment. Organizations such as the environment committees of the various chambers of commerce and the Private-sector Committee on the Environment review and comment on proposed government initiatives (or the lack of them) to address specific problems. Such comments often call on the government to do more, though with a stress on efficient policy approaches (i.e. greater use of economic incentives, standard setting, and monitoring without specific technology mandates), and with a stress on greater transparency and wider public participation in environmental policy-making.

At the same time, the shift in sovereignty represents an excellent opportunity to encourage the government to re-evaluate its vision for Hong Kong's economic future and the infrastructure plans necessary to realize this vision. If the new administration seeks to slow these enormously costly and potentially risky investments, it may well give increased attention to the under-examined and under-debated environmental impact of the developments.

The hope is that, in the longer term, there will be a growing sense of shared purpose between the government and the people, including the business community, with regard to development and the environment, engendering greater openness on the part of government toward decision-making on these and other fronts.

Select Bibliography

Arndt, H. W., 'Industrial Policy in East Asia', *Industry and Development*, 22 (1987): 1–66.

Arnott, R., 'Time for Revisionism on Rent Control?' *Journal of Economic Perspectives*, 9, 1 (1995): 99–120.

Barron, W., 'Evaluating Transport and Industrial Opinions in Hong Kong', *Energy Policy*, 21, 6 (1993): 679–90.

Barron, W., Lui, J., Lam, T., Wong, C., Peters, J., and Hedley, A., 'Benefits and Costs of an Air Quality Improvement: initial indications from an intervention in Hong Kong', *Contemporary Economic Policy*, 13, 4 (1995): 105–117.

Betson, C., and Liu, J., *Air Pollution and Respiratory Health in Primary School Children in Hong Kong, 1989–92: Report to the Environmental Protection Department*, Hong Kong, Government Printer, 1993.

Card, D., and Krueger, A. B., 'Minimum Wages and Employment: A Case Study of the Fast-Food Industry in New Jersey and Pennsylvania', *American Economic Review*, 84, 4 (1994): 772–793.

Castells, M., Goh, L., and Kwok, R. Y.-W., *The Shek Kip Mei Syndrome: Economic Development and Public Housing in Hong Kong and Singapore*. London, Pion Books, 1990.

Caves, R. E., 'Industrial Policy and Trade Policy: A Framework', in Mutoh, Sekiguchi, Suzumura, and Tamazawa (eds.) *Industrial Policies for Pacific Economic Growth*, Sydney, Allen and Unwin, 1986.

Chau, T. H., 'Address', *Proceedings of the International Conference on Fair Trading*, Hong Kong, Consumer Council, 1995.

Chow, T. S., 'Economic Restructuring and Services to Employees Affected: The Work of the Employees Retraining Board in Hong Kong', Paper presented to the Conference on Changing Employment Environments and the Development and Management of Human Resources. Hong Kong, Centre of Asian Studies, Hong Kong University, 1993.

Chen, E. K. Y., Wong, Teresa Y. C., and Wong Po-wah, 'The Hong Kong Economy at the Crossroads', *Asia Club Papers*, Tokyo Club Foundation for Global Studies, No. 2, 1991.

Chen, E. K. Y., and Wong, Teresa Y. C., 'The Future Direction of Industrial Development in the Asian Newly Industrialized Economies', in Suh Jang-won (ed.), *Strategies for Industrial Development: Concept and Policy Issues*, Asian and Pacific Development Centre and Korea Development Institute, 1989.

Coase, R., *The Firm, the Market, and the Law*, Chicago, University of Chicago Press, 1990.

Consumer Council, *Assessing Competition in the Domestic Water Heating and Cooking Fuel Market*, Hong Kong, Consumer Council, 1995.

Danziger, Z., Haveman, R., and Plotnick, R., 'How Income Transfer

Programs Affect Work, Savings, and Income Distribution: a Critical Review', *Journal of Economic Literature*, xix, 3 (1981): 975–1028.

Dasgupta, P., and Stoneman, P. (eds.), *Economic Policy and Technological Performance*, London, Cambridge University Press, 1987.

Eck, Alan, 'Job-related Education and Training: their impact on earnings,' *Monthly Labour Review* (October 1993): 21–38.

Economic Services Branch, *Container Terminal Development in Hong Kong Container Terminal 10 and 11 (CT 10 and CT 11)*, Hong Kong, Government Printer, 1995.

Environmental Protection Department, *Environment Hong Kong 1989 and years to 1995*, Hong Kong, Government Printer, 1989–95.

Flemming, J. M., 'Domestic financial policies under fixed and under floating exchange rates', *IMF Staff Papers*, 9 (1962): 369–79.

Forrest, R., and Murie, A., *Selling the Welfare State: the privatisation of public housing*, London, Routledge, 1988.

Friends of The Earth Hong Kong, *Joint Press Release, Community Groups' Concerns Over Port Development*, Friends of the Earth Hong Kong, 1995.

Friends of The Earth Hong Kong, *Friends of the Earth's Concerns About the Lantau Port Development*, Friends of the Earth Hong Kong, 1995.

Government Information Services, *Hong Kong's Port and Airport Development Strategy: A Foundation For Growth*, Hong Kong, Government Printer, 1992.

Hamilton, Gary (ed.), *Business Networks and Economic Development in East and Southeast Asia*, Hong Kong, Centre of Asian Studies, The University of Hong Kong, 1991.

Hedley, A., Peters, J., Lam, T., Ong, S., Wong, C., Tam, A., Hills, P., and Barron, W., 'Hong Kong: can the dragon clean its nest?', *Environment*, 32 (1990): 17–20, 39–45.

Ho Lok Sang, 'Labour and Employment', in Sung Yun-wing and Lee Ming-kwan (eds.), *The Other Hong Kong Report 1991*, Hong Kong, Chinese University Press, 1991.

Ho Lok Sang, 'Labour and Employment', in Cheng, Joseph and Kwong, Paul (eds.), *The Other Hong Kong Report 1992*, Hong Kong, Chinese University Press, 1992.

Ho, Y. K., Scott, R. H., and Wong, K. A., (eds.), *The Hong Kong Financial System*, Hong Kong, Oxford University Press, 1991.

Hodgson, Gregor, 'The Environmental Impact of Marine Dredging In Hong Kong', *Geotechnics and the Environment 93*, Working Paper of the Hong Kong Institution of Engineers, 1993.

Hong Kong Housing Authority, *Annual Report 1993/4*.

Hong Kong Government, *Report of the Task Force on Land Supply and Property Prices*, Hong Kong, Government Printer, 1994.

Hong Kong Government, *Cleaner Air: Further Proposals To Reduce*

Emissions From Diesel Vehicles, A Consultation Paper, Hong Kong, Government Printer, 1995.

Hong Kong Government, *Hong Kong 1995*, Hong Kong, Government Printer, 1995.

Hong Kong Government, *Hong Kong's Port and Airport Development Strategy: a foundation for growth*, Hong Kong, Government Printer, 1992.

Hong Kong Government, Advisory Committee on Diversification, *Report of the Advisory Committee on Diversification*, Hong Kong, Government Printer, 1979.

Hong Kong Monetary Authority (ed.), *Monetary Management in Hong Kong*, 1994.

Hong Kong Monetary Authority (ed.), *The Practice of Central Banking in Hong Kong*, 1994.

Jao, Y. C., *Towards the Future: Hong Kong's Financial System in Transition*, Hong Kong, Joint Publishing Co., 1993.

Jenny, Frederic, 'Address' *Proceedings of the International Conference on Fair Trading*, Hong Kong, Consumer Council, 1995.

Lai, L. W. C., 'The Property Price Crisis', in McMillen, D., and Man, S. W. (eds.), *The Other Hong Kong Report 1994*, Hong Kong, Chinese University Press, 1994.

Loh, C., 'The Political Process and Environmental Management: The Political Changes Needed for Basic Environmental Improvement in Hong Kong', *The Asian Journal of Environmental Management*, 2, 2 (1994): 61–8.

Mundell, R. A., 'Capital Mobility and Stabilization Policy under Fixed and Flexible Exchange Rates', *Canadian Journal of Economics and Political Science*, 29 (1963): 475–85.

Neumark, David, and Wascher, W., *Minimum Wage Effects on Employment and School Enrollment*, NBER Working Paper No. 4679, Cambridge, National Bureau of Economic Research, 1994.

Neumark, David, and Wascher, W., 'Minimum Wage Effects on School and Work Transitions of Teenagers', *American Economic Review Papers and Proceedings*, 1995.

Ng, N., *An Assessment of Strategies for the Management of Plastic Bag Wastes in Hong Kong*, doctoral thesis, The Centre of Urban Planning and Environmental Management, The University of Hong Kong.

Nyaw Mee-kau, and Wong, Teresa Y. C. (eds.), *Industrial and Trade Development in Hong Kong*, Hong Kong, Centre of Asian Studies, The University of Hong Kong, 1991.

Oxfam, *Disempowerment and Empowerment — An Exploratory Study on Low-Income Households in Hong Kong*, Hong Kong, Oxfam, 1995.

Patten, C., *Address by the Governor at the Opening of the 1993/4 Session of the Legislative Council*, Hong Kong, Government Printer, 1993.

Patten, C., *Governor's Policy Speech 11 October 1995*, Hong Kong, Government Printer, 1995.

Planning Department, *Metroplan: The Selected Strategy*, Hong Kong, Government Printer, 1992.

Port Development Board, *Annual Report 1993/4*, Hong Kong, Government Printer, 1994.

Rating and Valuation Department, *Hong Kong Property Review 1995*. Hong Kong, Government Printer, 1995.

Riche, Norbert, 'Consumer Access to Consumption and Consumer Protection Against Unfair Contracts', in *Developing Consumer Law in Asia*, Hong Kong, Consumers International, 1994.

Shojiro, Tokunaga (ed.), *Japanese Foreign Investment and Asian Economic Interdependence*, Tokyo, Tokyo University Press, 1992.

Weiss, John (ed.), *Industry in Developing Countries: Theory, Policy and Evidence*, London, Routledge, 1988.

Wong, Teresa Y. C., 'Hong Kong's Manufacturing Industries: Transformations and Prospects', in Leung, B., and Wong, Y. C. (eds.), *25 Years of Social and Economic Development in Hong Kong*, Hong Kong, Centre of Asian Studies, The University of Hong Kong, 1994.

Wong, Teresa Y. C., and Kwong, K. S., 'The Role of Hong Kong in Asia's Regional Economic Growth and Development', in Ng Sek Hong and Lethbridge, David (eds.), *The Business Environment of Hong Kong* (3rd edition), Hong Kong, Oxford University Press, 1995.

Wong, R. Y. C., and Staley, S., 'Housing and Land' in Cheng, J. Y. S., and Kwong, P. C. K. (eds.), *The Other Hong Kong Report 1992*, Hong Kong, Chinese University Press, 1992.

World Bank, *World Development Report 1995*, New York, Oxford University Press, 1995.

Yee, L., *The Efficiency of the Charging System for Industrial Wastewater Management in Hong Kong*, doctoral thesis, The Centre of Urban Planning and Environmental Management, The University of Hong Kong, 1995.

Young, Alwyn, 'A Tale of Two Cities: Factor Accumulation and Technical Change in Hong Kong and Singapore', in National Bureau of Economic Research, *Macroeconomics Annual 1992*, London, NBER, 1992.

Index